Fundamentals *of* Sustainable Business

A Guide for the Next 100 Years

World Scientific Series on 21st Century Business

ISSN: 1793-5660

World Scientific Series on
21st Century
Business

4

Fundamentals *of* Sustainable Business

A Guide for the Next 100 Years

Matthew Tueth
Aquinas College, USA

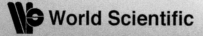
World Scientific

NEW JERSEY · LONDON · SINGAPORE · BEIJING · SHANGHAI · HONG KONG · TAIPEI · CHENNAI

Published by

World Scientific Publishing Co. Pte. Ltd.

5 Toh Tuck Link, Singapore 596224

USA office: 27 Warren Street, Suite 401-402, Hackensack, NJ 07601

UK office: 57 Shelton Street, Covent Garden, London WC2H 9HE

British Library Cataloguing-in-Publication Data
A catalogue record for this book is available from the British Library.

World Scientific Series on 21st Century Business — Vol. 4
FUNDAMENTALS OF SUSTAINABLE BUSINESS
A Guide for the Next 100 Years

ISBN-13 978-981-283-932-9
ISBN-10 981-283-932-1

Typeset by Stallion Press
Email: enquiries@stallionpress.com

This book is dedicated to the natural world that continues to support, inspire, and teach us and to the many people who recognize its splendor.

Preface

Fundamentals of Sustainable Business was written for students, business persons, and all others who are curious about the topic of sustainable business and are looking for a clear, thorough, and intriguing overview of this movement. Although previous books discuss certain aspects of sustainability, *Fundamentals of Sustainable Business* provides a comprehensive outline of the often misunderstood and over-simplified topic of sustainable business. This book offers considerable insight into the relatively new and compelling approach to human enterprise. Whether you are an ardent environmentalist, an ultra-conservative business owner, or somewhere in between, this book challenges a number of common and fundamental beliefs about the relationship between the natural world and human endeavor. It does not merely suggest an adjustment of conventional business assumptions or environmental theory, but rather outlines a radical departure from these traditional and seemingly disparate ideologies and proffers a unified and congruent body of thought. This book considers the problems *of* business, not simply the problems *in* business.

We will depart from traditional environmental and business perspectives so that you may consider some of the biggest challenges facing humankind from a different, and perhaps unfamiliar, perspective. The extensive economic, environmental, and social problems brought on by the first industrial revolution that have intensified over time are briefly reviewed but are not discussed in great detail in this text. Other books by contemporary authors such as Paul Hawken, Amory and Hunter Lovins, and William McDonough have previously documented this increasingly troubling predicament. Rather, this book concentrates on describing a shift from our current path of undermining vital support systems to a legacy of long-term opportunity and prosperity. People from a wide variety of experiences, perspectives, and places have already begun to embrace this extraordinary movement, and hopefully, an even more diverse fabric of society will continue to discover its relevance and value.

Let us turn our attention to our own lives for a moment to examine the movement's relevance to that situation. Most adults work long and hard in a variety of ways to earn a living and to perhaps even support a family. Although many of us enjoy our chosen professions, nearly all of us look forward to our free time spent in a variety of pleasurable activities. Family and friends may be high on such a list of activities, along with travel, the theater, music, books, movies, sporting events, exercise, camping, and even service to church or community. Our education, life experiences, and personal likes and dislikes all influence the free-time activities we select. Even though the amount of leisure time inside many developed nations has been shrinking for the past several decades, our free-time pursuits remain very important to us and to the quality of our lives.[1]

Our material belongings also influence the quality of our lives because they enable us to reside comfortably in our homes, travel to distant places, communicate with others, and enjoy a relatively comfortable life. Most readers of this book likely have a large inventory of possessions including vehicles, furniture, appliances, electronic devices, clothes, and recreational equipment. We have access to nearly unlimited retail product and service options, for example, a regional mall for clothing, a super-store for electronics, and grocery stores or restaurants for food. We have come to expect fully stocked store shelves and easily accessed e-businesses offering endless products via the Internet. Products at these outlets appear limitless, and only our cash supply or credit availability seems to restrict our purchases.

Spiritual considerations aside, what provides your material possessions and makes your enjoyable free-time activities possible? A common answer to this question might be simply the business sector. The worldwide industrial infrastructure extracts, processes, manufactures,

---

[1] See Jacobs and Gerson (2001) for an elaboration of these trends.

and markets the goods and services that global consumers desire. But a closer look at this question begs further consideration: what actually *supplies* the raw materials and energy that must feed the myriad of industrial processes? Consider that whether you live in Bangkok, Thailand, or Bar Harbor, Maine, every human endeavor, project, and activity is made possible directly by the natural world. Whether you enjoy rap music, classical music, walks on the beach, walks down Fifth Avenue, gourmet meals, Big Macs, television, cell phones, the company of family and friends, or simply relaxing and breathing — the natural world continually provides all the essential materials and energy for life on Earth. For example, green plants are the only entity on Earth that captures incoming solar energy and stores it in the chemical bonds of simple sugars; through this process, they release oxygen, a vital component of the air. In short, the entire animal kingdom, including man, *entirely depends* upon green plants for food to eat and oxygen to breathe. No other source for these two vital commodities exists. Green plants also help to maintain global and local climates, make habitat available for wildlife, build soil fertility and reduce erosion, muffle urban noise, offer shade and wind protection, provide the basis for many dozens of medicines, and generally beautify the planet.

Today most of us go about our lives breathing, drinking, eating, working, and recreating, all the while taking for granted the abundant oxygen, clean water, beauty, and food available to us. Americans typically are not aware at a conscious level of our dependence upon the natural world for the things we need and the things we enjoy most in our daily lives. The combination of the prodigious retail and marketing sectors and the lack of understanding of environmental principles in all levels of education also contribute substantially toward a developed world culture largely ignorant of the *vital role* of the natural world in our everyday lives. Not surprisingly, this constantly reinforced environmental disconnect translates into a general apathy for the natural world. Another commonly held supposition is that the natural world has an unlimited capacity to continue to provide us with everything we need and want and to absorb the various types and levels of industrial assaults and pollution.

Some of us may also be surprised to learn that the *way* our industrial systems meet our physical needs also *unnecessarily* depletes resources, puts persistent toxins into the biosphere, and results in global climate change, thereby decreasing options for future generations of world residents. The lack of recognition of the link between human prosperity and a healthy natural world has fostered an industrial system that still provides the goods and services we want in the immediate future but also brings momentous long-term negative consequences for all life on Earth. After briefly framing this unfortunate reality in Chapter 1, *Fundamentals of Sustainable Business* then concentrates on a new approach of solution-oriented systemic innovations that have begun to solve these dilemmas and offer rational hope for an abundant and healthy future.

Let's now turn our attention to the situation of personal transportation in the U.S. Gasoline today costs approximately eight times what it did just 35 years ago and, even when adjusted for inflation, a substantial price increase influences the transportation habits of many middle- and lower-class Americans. Had the automobile industry originally chosen a perpetually abundant and clean source of energy such as sunlight and then continuously improved a technology to support this selection, both the price and cost (they are in fact quite different) of personal transportation would be far less today, as would the climate-warming emissions from humanity's massive vehicle fleet.

But rising energy prices, tailpipe pollution, and a changing global climate are not the only undesirable results of our transportation technology of choice. We consistently use materials for the interior of our vehicles that release volatile toxins during the first year of ownership (yes, that new car smell) and subject riders to chronic inhalation of harmful contaminates. Owners of new cars are mostly unaware of this insidious assault on their bodies, or if aware, they may simply accept these conditions and consider these harmful effects as an unavoidable price of affluence. We also find that similar tragic consequences accompany numerous other products we use, from hospital intravenous (IV) tubes to carpeting to baby toys. Most of these isolated toxic exposures do not cause serious health problems alone, but the combined effects from dozens of minor (and completely unnecessary as we will see) day-to-day exposures pose significant threats to human health.

The following chapters present a truly revolutionary approach to business that has the capacity to *concurrently* produce long-term profitable businesses and local jobs, build healthy and vibrant communities, and enhance the natural world. We will examine a new paradigm for communities and organizations that a growing group of innovative business leaders around the world have already begun to embrace and implement. We will discuss the work of a number of visionary commercial pioneers that have set the tumblers in motion for this next industrial revolution. In the development of this new strategy, we will study an energy and materials system that has over 3.85 billion years of unprecedented success. We will learn how to build lasting value and wealth for ourselves, for future generations, and for all other species henceforth by our everyday actions at home, at work, and even during our leisure time.

Does this optimistic scenario sound too good to be true? This movement has already begun in many places around the world and has become, among other things, a considerable advantage for involved businesses and communities. This book summarizes the most salient work of leading visionaries in the sustainable business movement and introduces some original concepts as well. I ask that you read the following chapters with an open mind, allowing your imagination free reign. I encourage you to prepare to challenge and reshape a number of your basic beliefs and trust your intuition rather than rely on your past practices throughout the process. Realize that remodeling a personal paradigm is often uncomfortable, but at the same time such a conversion can be immensely rewarding. Expect your perspective of modern life to change during and after reading this solution-oriented text, and expect to find the experience startling, logical, and captivating. Most importantly, do not be surprised to find yourself drawn toward a more satisfying and engaging relationship with your community, the natural world, and business, which may inspire new personal contributions from you that will aid in the transformation of humans into a positive force on our planet for all time.

The following is a preview of what we can expect as we move through *Fundamentals of Sustainable Business*. First, an initial short summary of the adverse effects of commerce since the first industrial revolution is presented. Several serious flaws of conventional business are briefly discussed as well as problems in the natural world and our own communities that were brought on by these failings. We examine the subsequent emergence of *a movement from inside business* that has begun to direct organizations to more effective and positive activities. As we will see, this new approach gives us a framework to simultaneously advance business, the natural world, and human communities.

Both our energy and material processes are thoroughly discussed and reconsidered. We reflect on the most intelligent source for help with the key changes inside business and why this consultant holds such promise for humankind. Stories of cutting-edge businesses of all sizes, types, and locations in the sustainable business movement are featured along with metrics to measure success. We consider the appropriate roles of specific business positions as well as the function of higher education and of government in this movement. In the face of current globalization trends, we examine the possible evolution of regional communities into healthy, diverse, abundant, self-sufficient, and beautiful places for countless generations to grow and prosper. Finally, obstacles to this transformation and the lurking pitfalls that could impede its progress are explained and considered.

I congratulate you on your decision to explore the ideas contained in these chapters. Students of all ages who consider the themes found in *Fundamentals of Sustainable Business* react in a variety of ways to the experience. As an educator in this regard, I have known many people who have described the experience as an *epiphany* — business people who now thrive by putting these principles into practice, consumers who contribute by reassessing and redirecting what they buy and whom they patronize, and college students who follow their new passion in the preparation for their professional careers. Many of these engaged citizens choose to lobby their political leaders to work for positive changes in policy directives.

At the same time, some seasoned business folk find it difficult to accept these ideas in their entirety, owing in part perhaps to their reluctance to acknowledge personal complicity in the insidious tragedies of business as usual. Others lack the familiarity and understanding of the natural world and how our industrial activities systematically degrade the planet. Still other experienced adults accept and internalize the tenets of this movement and very quickly become impassioned supporters. But no matter which perspective you bring to the table, this book will provide a compelling and stimulating journey through a variety of dilemmas and solutions that offer previously unimagined outcomes for business, the natural world, and human communities. The extent to which this reading experience produces a change in perspective and generates action is personal and dynamic. Some readers may find that they intuit huge implications and changes generated by this body of thought gradually. In fact, if you read this book a second time, the principles outlined herein may resonate even deeper with you and provide an even more enjoyable and rewarding experience.

Your background and life experiences no doubt helped to motivate your curiosity in this movement; actually, the foundation of my involvement with sustainable business is also rooted in the distant past. I grew up in the 1950s and 60s in the industrial town of Alton, Illinois located on the banks of the Mississippi River just north of St. Louis, Missouri. My mother's standing rules were that her boys (my two older brothers and I) play *outside every summer day* (unless it was raining) and walk over a mile across town to and from our grade school and high school. Because of her edicts, I regularly landed in Alton's many parks and woods and at the river's edge.

One bright summer day I was climbing up and over a variety of dead tree snags along the banks of Old Man River when I noticed a curious tan rock about the size of one of my mom's chocolate chip cookies half buried in the riverbank sand. After extracting and washing off my prize, I noticed two curious markings on one side of the rock. Unable to interpret their meanings, I ran about five minutes back into town to Haynor Public Library. I carried my find into the geology section and in about 45 minutes, to my amazement, I found an illustration of a nearly identical rock in a book of fossils. The text confirmed it as a fossil of a freshwater fish. I returned home later that afternoon and carefully wrapped this treasure in one of my father's old rags and placed it gently among my other priceless finds of petrified wood, broken arrowheads, and various other unidentified rock specimens for later examination in my childhood leisure. This attention-commanding experience was fairly typical of a long line of magically satisfying everyday events that the outdoors continued to provide in my youth. Clearly, nature was a fountainhead of wonders and mysteries for this ordinary Midwestern boy.

After graduating from high school in 1971, keenly aware of my affinity for the outdoors, I earned a bachelor's degree in wildlife management from Southern Illinois University at Carbondale. I spent the better part of 1977 working near Mt. St. Helens for the U.S. Forest Service in the Gifford Pinchot National Forest of Washington State; I missed the violent 1980 volcanic eruption by only a few geological seconds. In my next 20 professional years, I worked in the outdoors again, this time employed by the Illinois Department of Natural Resources.

Firmly ensconced inside the State of Illinois workforce and heading for full retirement in 2013, I was drawn to pursue a master's degree in environmental studies at the Edwardsville campus of Southern Illinois University. A graduate degree in my lifelong passion would hopefully fill in the gaps left by my casual but consistent efforts to improve my understanding of the natural world and how humans relate to it. After completing two years of evening classes and a thesis that concentrated on contemporary sustainability issues, I graduated in May 1997.

Seizing on the opportunity to maintain academic momentum and commit professional suicide, I resigned my enjoyable and reasonably lucrative position with the State of Illinois and intrepidly began the pursuit of a Ph.D. in environmental science at Oklahoma State University in Stillwater. With my deep curiosity about man's relationship to the natural world and a newfound passion to teach, I spent the next three years enrolled in doctoral courses, teaching undergraduate courses, and working diligently on my dissertation research project. I successfully passed my comprehensive exams and defended my dissertation research, which dealt with sustainability factors in ancient civilizations, and graduated in May 2000.

I accepted an assistant professor position at the beautifully wooded campus of Aquinas College in Grand Rapids, Michigan and began my life as a tenure-track professor in August 2000. Just as I was firmly committed to teaching environmental studies and geography, another life-changing opportunity appeared. The Aquinas provost (a former history professor and the current president of the college) called a meeting with the business and science faculty in the fall of 2002 and asked if anyone had an interest in developing a new academic concentration involving environmental studies, science, and business. Looking around the room, the provost saw that no hands were raised, except for the new environmental studies professor in the back row. The provost thanked everyone for attending and promptly dismissed the meeting.

Thankfully, no one in the room noticed that I was dumbstruck. I remember the situation as surreal; had I misheard or misinterpreted what had just happened? — The subject had just been raised to develop an *interdisciplinary* program involving business and environmental science! Throughout my undergraduate and graduate academic careers I had always believed that the theme of higher education to emphasize single-discipline learning was not in the best interest of life on Earth (my undergraduate professors nearly always disagreed). Swirling around in my head for years was the notion that a plethora of important connections exists between the physical sciences, social sciences, humanities, business, and the natural environment, and that many of these relationships had not been identified, explored, and emphasized by academia. So, when this pivotal meeting ended, with my mind racing, I gathered myself and chased after the provost until I caught him just as he was leaving the science building. Breathing heavily by this time I said "Sir, I really think you are on to something here. I have dreamed of putting something like this together, but never did I think that such a chance would come." He responded, "Apparently none of your colleagues see much value in this." "Don't worry about that" I said naively, "I know we can make this work. " The next week he called me into his office and asked me to organize and lead this new interdisciplinary program.

And so my sustainable business odyssey began. I learned that a number of business leaders in West Michigan were already pioneering ways to link profits, people, and the planet. I contacted these forward thinkers and invited them to discuss the design of a new academic program that would provide our graduates with an expertise in conventional business, physical science, and environmental studies, as well as with a new approach to business. Most of these inimitable professionals graciously agreed, and together we set out to develop a program that would provide a training ground for undergraduates in this new approach to business.

Many considerations were a part of the forthcoming academic design process: the interdependencies between man and nature, the key components of thriving human communities, the need to provide a competitive financial advantage for participants, and the intention to pass along a better world to future generations of all species. The challenge was indeed formidable but our group was knowledgeable, passionate, and committed.

These anecdotes are some of the background circumstances behind my involvement in the sustainable business movement. Further, having two daughters and two granddaughters motivates me to work as an educator for positive change for the future. I am sure you have your own personal stories and a rich mixture of reasons for considering all or part of the paradigm shift presented in the following chapters. Nature is filled with rich diversity and countless inter-relationships among all members, and the sustainable business revolution is taking shape in a similar fashion. A variety of people in many parts of the world are independently beginning to redesign business and to find remedies for many of the existing core problems of commerce.

Matthew W. Tueth

Acknowledgements

The author thanks the Steelcase foundation for its gracious and generous support of this project, and offers special thanks to former board trustee Peter M. Wege for his many contributions to a healthy and bountiful West Michigan.

The author thanks Aquinas College President C. Edward Balog for his continuous leadership, support, and confidence.

The author thanks student worker Mariel Borgman for her assistance during the completion of this work.

The author thanks his longtime friend Jim for inspiration in the earliest stages of this project.

The author lovingly thanks his wife, Maggie, for her patience and support during the many months of work that spilled into our private time and for her countless hours of editing and advisement.

Contents

Chapter 1

Houston, We Have a Problem

The U.S. is the third most populated nation in the world, behind only China and India, and is home to over 300 million people. The recent increase in population in the U.S. is due to immigration from many locations around the globe. The U.S. is third only to Russia and Canada in total land area, and still holds substantial natural resources including farmland, timber, metals, coal, and even crude oil. The abundant supply of useable raw materials has greatly contributed to U.S. prosperity for hundreds of millions of people for more than two centuries. Although the U.S. still has considerable poverty, crime, and economically depressed areas within its borders, the standard of living enjoyed in most U.S. communities is significantly higher than the day-to-day reality for billions of people throughout the developing world.

Over the past 200 years, our nation has developed an extensive industrial complex to provision food, transportation, shelter, and various industrial products for over ten generations of Americans. Today the U.S. accounts for approximately 20% of global natural resource consumption with only 4.5% of the world's population. In spite of some negative international sentiment toward America, many people from around the world try any means available to enter our nation and start a new life on U.S. soil. Even though many of these attempts are unsuccessful, desperate individuals repeatedly continue their efforts. In contrast, most Americans enjoy a high standard of living, and today few U.S. citizens choose to emigrate in search of more promising lives abroad. The U.S. has always offered exceptional quality-of-life opportunities for its residents that are unavailable in most other nations.

The continued expansion of the U.S. industrial complex over the past century has indeed provided the means for considerable economic prosperity. The unique heritage of capitalism, democracy, natural resource availability, and diverse human spirit has enabled a standard of living envied by many around the world. This heritage includes an immense economy that today is targeted by most major international manufacturers and investors as a lucrative market for products and a reliable location for speculative ventures. But a complete accounting of our economic legacy also includes a dark side. Not only has U.S. industry provided a dependable stream of goods and services, but it has also contributed a laundry list of serious problems for humanity and most biota, including an increase of cancer and other major health threats, loss of domestic jobs, decreasing soil fertility, a variety of compromised natural systems, and global climate change (discussed in greater detail later). We shall see how these pernicious health, environmental, social, and economic realities that have accompanied industrial expansion are seriously regrettable and, for the most part, unnecessary.

1.1 Our Early Approach to Mounting Problems

By the middle of the 19th century, many American cities had become dirty, noisy, polluted, and congested places to live, work, and raise a family. Rural areas were also fraught with serious quality-of-life issues. By this time, agricultural soil fertility was decreasing and soil erosion was increasing, and not long after World War II ended, the new petroleum-based pesticides were touted as the linchpin of a productive agricultural system. During this period of increasingly apparent environmental troubles, a few ardent advocates organized and supported various causes including wilderness, wildlife, soil, water, forests, prairies, and pollution reduction. These early impassioned advocacy groups mostly acted independently of one another, championing their own single causes and finding only limited success influencing meaningful public policy changes that benefited their agendas.

In 1962, Rachel Carson's book *Silent Spring* was published, and it became a lightning rod for the myriad of environmental causes existing at that time. Her timely message, an indictment of the pesticide industry as a major polluter, fused many independent advocacy factions into a single, cohesive, and identifiable "modern environmental movement," allowing this new societal cause to quickly develop into a formidable force for change. A new appreciation and respect for nature began appearing in the public mainstream as did an increasing concern for how American urbanization negatively affects the health of humans and of the natural world. New champions of nature called "environmentalists" began to take a respected place within academia, government, and non-profit organizations. Grassroots movements led by these environmentalists flourished, and their ideals were even incorporated into national platforms of political parties. The original Clean Air Act, the Environmental Policy Act, and the new federal bureau called the Environmental Protection Agency were among the tangible results to surface in the early 1970s in the U. S. as a direct result of this robust environmental movement. The cause for *reducing* the harmful effects of business upon society and nature had now taken hold, and this commitment was illustrated by a number of regulatory attempts by federal and state government to *slow down* industry's seeming indiscriminate efforts to increase its profits at the expense of environmental quality.

Historically, these environmentalists generally viewed leaders of industry as self-serving, dishonest, and dangerous; they lobbied state and federal lawmakers to legislate environmental policies that coerced business to conform to the environmentalist agenda. Business leaders, in turn, viewed environmentalists as impractical extremists, whose unreasonable demands would raise the costs of goods and services, thereby putting many companies out of business, increasing the U.S. unemployment rate, and lower the overall standard of living. Over the past 40 years, both sides have dug in their heels, resisted compromise, and operated within an evolving national environmental policy framework that has cost business and consumers billions of dollars per year but has not significantly mitigated the root problems. Despite many earnest attempts by legislators to craft effective U.S. environmental law since the 1960s, we continue (unnecessarily) to systematically poison ourselves (albeit at a slower rate), lose domestic jobs, and dismantle many of our once-thriving local communities.

1.2 Our Problems Continue

Since the 1960s, concerned U.S. citizens have generally looked to government to remedy this deteriorating quality-of-life situation, but our public servants have not been up to the task. One endemic but seldom cited hindrance is that our legislators and executive office holders are held accountable for their public service performance during relatively short terms of office and, not surprisingly, they routinely avoid tackling the core causes of problems that will provide the majority of benefits far into the future. Unfortunately in our political system, reactionary and short-sighted legislative action that generates headlines for the next re-election campaign is the more common reality. At the same time, Americans have tolerated this approach to issues by politicians and, for the most part, have not demonstrated a mandate for effective systemic change in this regard. We will discuss considerably more about government's role and responsibility in the sustainable business movement in Chapter 6.

In short, this insidious and protracted industrial tyranny shortens the lives of our citizens, undermines our economic stability, and continuously degrades the very natural systems upon which all life depends. Exacerbating the situation is an insufficient understanding and appreciation by most citizens of our reliance upon the natural world and the myriad of vital services that come from it. Most of us still envision a mythical inexhaustible supply of raw materials from nature and her limitless capacity for absorbing all the toxic punches we can throw at her. Unfortunately, today we find most K-through-12 school systems lacking comprehensive and integrated *environmental and social-based curricula,* and this deficiency fuels our disassociation of human prosperity and natural world health. Most of us simply do not recognize the irreplaceable benefits provided by only a healthy and prolific natural environment, such as oxygen production, climate stabilization, water purification, flood control, soil fertility, materials for our products, and aesthetic beauty. Anyone who has difficulty grasping this concept needs only to consider the single source of the oxygen in that last breath of air just inhaled (green plants).

When asked to describe our *community,* loosely defined as where we routinely get our needs met, we might include our town, neighborhood, or section of city where we work and live, but rarely do we consider the surrounding natural world in this context. Particularly for those of us living in urban settings, nature is commonly viewed as a peripheral and non-essential part of our existence that we occasionally visit, sometimes only out of necessity to get to a destination, other times by choice for some type of outdoor recreational activity such as camping, hiking, or boating. In the mid-1940s, visionary Aldo Leopold wrote in the last chapter of his book *A Sand County Almanac* that the natural course for humanity is to expand our concept of community (and ethics) to include "... soils, waters, plants, and animals ...." Our continuing failure to recognize the significance and value of a healthy natural environment in our personal life and in business is myopic and dangerous. Since we tend to take care of only those things we value, our extended legacy of natural world destruction is not particularly surprising. Unfortunately, this prolonged oversight has placed all humanity in a seriously compromised situation.

Perhaps just as important, in addition to the lack of appreciation of the natural world by the average citizen, many environmental advocates have failed to recognize the importance of a vibrant and durable *industrial sector* to provide a high quality of life and a heritage of opportunity for future human generations. Aggravating the situation is the preponderance of business managers today who pursue this myopic quest to increase short-term profits, much to the detriment of long-term economic health and stability. A far too speculative mortgage market or the corporate takeover and subsequent dismantling of successful businesses are examples of this sort of near-sighted, self-centered behavior. Also consider that for the past several decades, U. S. manufacturing companies have continually increased the amount of foreign-made components in order to reduce production costs, and consumers consistently chase down low-priced foreign goods at corporate "big box" retail stores with little or no consideration of the comprehensive effects this purchasing pattern has on their communities.

When more local dollars leave a region for goods and services than come into that region, an insidiously negative trade-deficit result comes into play. When we patronize corporate restaurants, food producers, banks, fast food chains, or clothing stores for example, we send our money to distant supply chains and profits to worldwide stockholders. This methodical loss of wealth sucks the life blood of jobs and financial capital from regions throughout the country. We unwittingly allow an economic pattern to continue where locally generated wealth exits a region unnecessarily. A better option is to become aware of some of the many outstanding locally owned businesses within your community and to patronize them frequently. In addition to enjoying establishments of unique character, product, and personal service, more of your money spent at locally owned businesses stays in your community to re-circulate. Studies suggest that out of every $100 spent at locally owned businesses, at least $25 more remains in the local economy when compared to businesses that are not locally owned.[2]

One of the easiest ways to begin to support local businesses while improving the value received is to patronize the variety of local restaurants available in a community. Often this interesting and ethnically diverse collection of eateries offers more appealing food, service, and total dining experience when compared to the chain establishments. Another way to support local businesses is to browse the local farmers markets and food cooperatives that are popping up all over the U.S. Similar opportunities to support local business exist in many communities for entertainment, business services, grocery, real estate, and retail clothing. Remember, too, that a marketplace with many small businesses encourages fair competition, innovation, and the best value for the consumer's dollars.

City, county, and even state governments have the opportunity to enact policy that incentivizes local and regional businesses and discourages the loss of local jobs and wealth. Unfortunately, many of our current economic policy makers still do not recognize the long-term value provided by a *locally owned and anchored regional business sector*. Often foreign-owned companies are seen by government as the brass ring to snare, and officials use huge tax breaks and public infrastructure improvements to try and lure these international facilities while upping the ante for other U.S. cities hoping to attract overseas

---

[2] See Cunningham, Houston, and Sheppard (2004).

businesses. However, the short-term political and social benefits of a new foreign facility is more than negated by the lack of tax revenues for the local school systems and the eventual loss of jobs from the corporation pulling up stakes when they find another location that offers them more favorable tax, wage, and infrastructure concessions. This scenario with its not-so-happy ending has played out countless times in recent decades in the U.S., and still, headline-chasing politicians continue to concentrate limited economic development dollars on foreign industry rather than on local community efforts. This dog-chasing-its-tail strategy is not part of the sustainable business movement. The role of government in advancing a transition to healthy and stable local economies is extensively discussed in Chapter 6.

1.3 Early Visionaries and the Resistance to Change

A number of astute authors as early as the mid-20th century, including Aldo Leopold and Rachel Carson, published works that identified parts of the unsettling trend previously described and suggested systemic changes in our approach toward business, community, and the environment. Other "outside-the-box" thinkers such as California economist Garret Hardin, in addition to acknowledging portions of the aforementioned problems, expressed serious pessimism about the possibility for significantly changing our course.[3] In 1993, author Paul Hawken published the strikingly influential book *The Ecology of Commerce* in which he not only identified industry as culpable in our dire state of affairs but more importantly recognized the unique opportunity and power of business to lead meaningful long-term recovery rather than governments or non-profit organizations. Hawken deftly points out that our problems are entrenched throughout commerce and that a consequential solution involves a fundamental redesign by business itself. Later we will also discuss the original contributions to this movement from other visionaries such as Janine Benyus, Amory and Hunter Lovins, Sandra Steingraber, Michael Shuman, William McDonough, and Michael Braungart.

---

[3] See Hardin (1968) for a harsh but convincing pessimistic argument.

The unconventional nature of the strategies covered in these chapters require considerable thought and time to process and integrate into our paradigm. On a personal level, many find the requisite professional self-examination particularly challenging in a number of ways. First, those who are professionally and personally successful are not always inclined to seriously reconsider basic components of their core belief system. The necessary open-minded self-scrutinizing re-examination is difficult and unpleasant, and so many of us avoid it. Second, after acquiring a basic understanding of the natural world and the adverse effects upon it and ourselves by business as usual, we often have difficulty accepting complicity of our own professional activities. We may discover an internal dilemma in admitting that we have spent a good portion of our lives indirectly weakening future prospects for the natural world and for our grandchildren alike.

The final requirement of a paradigm shift involves one's own personal time and effort, a most precious commodity. Most Americans lead quite busy lives integrating family, job, friends, and personal interests. Simply finding the time to read this book may be difficult for you, let alone finding the time to consider the far-reaching ramifications of its tenets and to apply them in your life. However, we do attend to the things that are most important to us, and you may find that the most onerous option will be to *not* follow your intuition and heart down this unsettled road of change. At any rate, we will fix only what we know to be broken, so let's go a bit deeper into humankind's situation.

1.4 Do Current Free-Market Mechanisms Help?

Today environmental scientists around the world constantly gather data and monitor various types of pollution, habitat degradation, and natural resource exploitation. Considering the enormity of our global industrial activities and the corresponding negative effects upon life on Earth, it is fairly easy to understand how business is often viewed by the investigator as the incorrigible ecological villain. The 1984 Union Carbide chemical plant disaster in Bhopal, India; the 1986 meltdown and explosions of the Chernobyl, Ukraine nuclear reactor;

and the 1989 Exxon Valdez oil tanker calamity in Prince William Sound of southeastern Alaska are three well-publicized examples of catastrophic industrial debacles.

For decades environmentalists and social reformers have pushed for a strong set of state and federal environmental regulations that *force* business to reduce the contamination of air, water, and soils and to limit the exploitation of limited natural resources. As discussed earlier, this approach simply has not worked well through time for the environment or for world citizens. Even with billions of dollars spent by government and business to mitigate these problems through a labyrinth of complex environmental regulations, each year the U.S. alone still releases millions of pounds of persistent toxins and generates thousands of tons of lethal high-level nuclear waste, some of which will require secure storage for tens of thousands of years.[4] A closer look also reveals that many exploitive industrial practices continue, such as the indiscriminate harvest of tropical rain forest timber, that significantly weaken a variety of natural systems upon which humans and all other life depend.

In theory, both U.S. business and consumers rely on our modified market-based economic system to appropriately adjust prices and demand for natural resources. Commonly, when supplies of a particular resource dwindle and the price for this resource subsequently rises, we rely on technology advancements to improve our utilization efficiency, to locate a new source for that resource, or to discover a suitable substitute for that resource, all of which cause prices to fall back to lower levels. Unfortunately, a variety of free-market system defects exists in this scenario, including the following: people other than the buyer routinely pay part of the cost of goods or services because of the pervasive externalizing effects of pollution (electric bill), certain essential commodities have no substitutes (oxygen), most essential services have no substitutes (favorable climate), legal monopolies do exist (utility companies), government does regulate certain types of commerce (banking industry), government provides

---

[4] See Walker, Hopkin, Sibly, and Peakall (2006) for this and other numerous pertinent pollution statistics.

billions of dollars in subsidies for certain types of resource extraction (metals and crude oil), and the value of natural capital (biodiversity) and natural services (pollination of crops) is largely unaccounted for and ignored by the market.

To further hamstring the effectiveness of our economic system, we monitor domestic financial activities using misleading indicators that do not scrutinize the long-term effects of industry on both human and natural communities. For example, our common economic indicators such as gross domestic product assume a dollar spent on our prison system provides the same value as a dollar spent on our educational system or a dollar spent on medical treatment of an ailment provides the same value as a dollar used for preventive health care. Our gross undervaluing of the natural world, the market failures of capitalism, and our inability to recognize and monitor useful economic information have put us in a situation where we covertly pass on harmful economic, environmental, and social consequences to people distant to us in both location and time, which is nothing short of a poignant non-stop dose of intergenerational tyranny. Ironically at the same time, we routinely allow short-sighted and relatively inconsequential issues to dominate mainstream media and public conversation while the issues of enormous repercussions described above remain on the sidelines.

Many well-intentioned social and economic reform efforts have historically focused on relieving the symptoms of our troubles rather than on an overhaul of the underlying systemic problems themselves. One example is the emphasis in our nation on combating illegal drug sales rather than on targeting the root causes for societal demand for such substances. Another example is government bailouts of failing industrial sectors such as the auto industry or commercial banking. These types of ill-advised policies squander billions of public dollars on symptoms of the problems without significantly affecting the core systemic issues that ultimately keep us permanently mired in the same untoward situations. If the same type of misdirected superficial approach is maintained for our current industrial dilemma, similar results can be expected. In short, nothing changes if nothing changes.

1.5 An Intelligent Beginning

Auspiciously, a fresh, systemic, solution-oriented approach has been quietly taking shape over the past couple of decades that leverages the inextricable links among business, society, and the natural world. Although this approach involves environmental themes, it is not merely a continuation of the well-intentioned but largely ineffective modern environmental movement. Rather than heavy-handed government regulators attempting to *coerce* business into specific actions or end results, this approach originates *inside business itself*. Instead of a bevy of regulatory requirements adding to the overall costs and complexity of doing business, this new strategy finds business, among other things, *improving* its economic performance. Leaders from all business sectors — extractive, processing, supply chain, manufacturing, service, and retail — and from all business sizes — sole proprietor to multinational corporations and for-profit companies to non-profit institutions — and even governmental departments have the opportunity to join their innovative and inspirational counterparts and begin the transformation of their own organization.

A word of warning to those whose interest is peaked: this movement is not about pulling the old recycling bins out of storage, turning down the office thermostat, or even meeting those government-mandated pollution and worker-safety regulations. As the coming chapters will explain, this movement involves a series of universal and sweeping changes in our approach to production and consumption of goods and services that will dramatically and positively affect the very core of business and society. Now let's review a bit of history concerning the evolution of our current *de facto* production systems.

The western industrial revolution began in northern England in the late 18th century and spawned new technologies that first produced textiles and later other goods in a superior fashion to previously existing methods. This new approach gradually proved to be a significant advantage over the simpler and less efficient technologies of the past and produced lower-cost goods that were then made available to a much larger market. But this revolution, led by early British industrialists, lacked an early long-term comprehensive design plan; the major single short-term goal was to provide British commerce a major advantage over other exporting nations. This technological revolution did achieve that goal, and Great Britain used its superior navy to firmly establish trade relationships for its manufactured items. Soon, this fresh industrial technology spread across political boundaries to continental Europe and the new fledgling United States of America.

Unfortunately, the fossil-fuel energy choices, linear cradle-to-grave material strategy, and unsavory working conditions have combined to also deliver a legacy of pollution-induced illness, short supplies of key production materials, denuded global farmland, and Russian-roulette-style global climate change risks that we pass on to our children. Clearly, this catastrophic endowment was not part of a plan crafted by industrialists throughout the recent past. Rather, the snowballing deleterious effects resulted from a lack of thoughtful and intelligent planning early in the revolution. Had early industrialists set their sights on *an industrial system that could indefinitely supply mankind the goods and services for a high quality of life,* our need for such a drastic and immediate change in course would not exist.

The leaders of today's sustainable business revolution have the opportunity to avoid the devastatingly unfortunate blunder of proceeding without an inspired and intelligent design plan. Fortunately, various key instigators of this new movement have begun by crafting innovation components that are intended to deliver only positive long- and short-term outcomes for all world community members. Momentum within the movement provides a growing opportunity to re-invent business into not only efficient, profit-driven enterprises but also to design organizations that are intentionally innovative, that restore the natural world, and that grow the local community as part of their day-to-day operations. Indeed, if our commercial enterprises are to have the capacity to continually support all humanity through time, deep environmental and social considerations are requirements, not options, for this *second industrial revolution.*

Incumbent upon this movement is to — once and for all — design the provisioning of consumers so that *all* outcomes of industry are positive and supportive for *all* life on Earth. Today we find that our current production strategies do not acknowledge or approach this criterion. For example, the production of common office white paper not only provides useful printing material but also requires the harvest of oxygen-producing, habitat-providing, and carbon-sequestering trees. The most common wood pulp bleaching process also emits into the air extremely dangerous carcinogens called dioxins and furans. Even the process for most white-paper reprocessing (generally referred to as "recycling" and considered environmentally friendly) unwittingly releases these same chemicals and uses fossil fuels to power the system.

However, the inadvertent but harmful consequences of white-paper production and reprocessing are not foregone conclusions. Chlorine-free processes exist today that do not emit dioxins while processing wood pulp or used white paper. Indeed, print surfaces exist today that use a reusable synthetic polymer material instead of a wood pulp base. These types of successful process innovation rely upon the creativity of savvy design teams who are committed to delivering high product performance at a reasonable price. Intelligently redesigned industrial processes provide value that will attract a broad base of consumers at the marketplace, particularly if the new product or service actually enhances product appearance and performance.

1.6 Are the Results Worth the Effort?

Many reasons exist for expanding our profit-driven commercial endeavors to include both natural world and societal considerations. In 1997, ecological economist Robert Costanza and a team of distinguished researchers documented the importance of the natural world as a fundamental form of capital for human society (and for the business of millions of other species as well).[5] The term *natural capital* includes living and non-living components of the environment that work in concert to produce beneficial conditions for all life on Earth, including a favorable climate, productive soils, and a materials cycling system throughout the biosphere. Unfortunately, the capacity of natural capital to provide these vital services is continuously degraded by

---

[5] See Costanza, *et al.* (1997) for a detailed accounting.

the many routine activities of industrialized man. Costanza and his research team recommend that business leaders recognize and acknowledge the value of the natural world and that industry actively engage the challenge of restoring and supporting all forms of natural capital just as business does with the more conventional types of capital such as its production machinery, office equipment, and buildings. Although natural capital is generally considered a *common property resource* (owned by no one but vital to all), clean air and clean water is just as essential to sustained positive business activity as privately held equipment or monetary wealth.

Another opportunity for substantial progress involves the treatment of employees and the relationship between employees and the organization. A growing number of business leaders have begun to recognize the direct payback for actively supporting their employees and communities in a variety of ways. Organizations typically invest substantial time and money to attract and continually train their staff, so long-term retention of skilled and satisfied employees in a productive work environment is a significant asset for business. Workers who are comfortable, properly equipped, and fairly compensated most often perform more productively and creatively and display loyalty to their companies.

Another opportunity for business involves cultivating interrelationships among the organization, its workforce, and the surrounding community. Movement-oriented business leaders have learned that circumstances benefitting their employees and communities also benefit their companies. They are finding that becoming more involved in the fabric of community life pays dividends in terms of recognition as solid community members and supporters of civic improvement. Another advantageous activity is cultivating mutually beneficial associations with other nearby businesses by combining resources for a common purpose such as group purchasing or by determining if one company's waste product could be an asset for another company. Chapter 4 discusses in detail business leaders that are particularly focused on developing strong support structures with their employees and the surrounding communities.

Philanthropic community involvement is a way that a business can improve the local living environment and its ability to attract and hold top employees. Often locally owned businesses with deeply established roots have a history of investing in and giving back to local communities, and subsequently they enjoy the long-term benefits of a more stable and productive workforce. Conversely, because corporations have philanthropic restraints placed on them by their corporate charters, inspired leaders sometimes will establish foundations with the role of allocating sizeable financial resources toward a variety of national, state, and local causes. Creative minds in both sets of circumstances have devised impressive community partnerships that help all parties involved.

Today, numerous examples of benevolent projects exist that benefit society, nature, and the organization. An endowment scholarship fund for low-income students who enroll in an undergraduate sustainable business program is an example of a particularly effective hybrid initiative that provides a critical cutting-edge education experience to those who otherwise very likely would not have this opportunity. The underwriting organization would then have an opportunity to advance its own efforts toward sustainable practices by providing internships for these students and then hiring the most promising interns to participate in the company transition. In addition to providing real value to the participating business, this ingenious program also benefits the natural world and the human community, and it offers the disadvantaged but talented students the opportunity to apply sustainable business theory in a real-world setting.

Let us now briefly turn our attention to an opportunity for improvement of the durable goods manufacturing sector. Product demand volatility is a constant challenge for supply-chain manufacturers and big-ticket item producers as well. Drastically reducing the frequency and intensity of the product demand changes (both downturns and upturns) can help stabilize a company's business operation and the size of its workforce. Cyclical expansion and contraction of a company's labor force in order to align with product demand is an expensive proposition for business and a negative influence for communities. In the next chapter we will discuss at length one particular about-face strategy that, among other things, works to significantly reduce the oscillating demand cycle for products over time, lower long-term production costs, decrease the extraction of raw materials, and stabilize community jobs.

For the past several decades, concerned citizens have looked toward government for relief from the litany of serious problems that accompany commercial endeavors, and most have been largely disappointed. A remaking of business by business with the outcome of simultaneously promoting profitability, people, and the planet is outlined in the following chapters. Today, manufacturing, engineering, architecture, construction, health care, and a variety of service sectors are already actively involved in the evolution of this movement. As we will see, government and our formal educational system also play important roles, and the *coordinated efforts* of all private, non-profit, and government sectors are needed to give this movement the best chance of lasting success.

Interestingly, sustainable business differs from previous social reform movements in that it lacks both a single visionary leader and a central location of origin; rather, it is inspired by an assortment of creative thinkers and doers throughout the western world and, in some ways, is linked to traditional Eastern thought. Many people from a variety of backgrounds and settings have started the ball rolling, and hopefully a much larger group will add to the current momentum of change and further champion this emerging revolution. But the maturation process of the movement is at a critical point in its early stage, and the next set of choices by engaged businesses will significantly influence the depth and intensity of these efforts.

We now face a sobering dilemma in the redesign process for commerce that most of us did not see coming. What guides do movement leaders use to ensure our best chance for success in this monumental planning process? Taking this question one step further and keeping in mind the track record of humanity the last few centuries, we ask ourselves if our best interests are served to assume that we have the ability to successfully transition to a thriving and sustainable society? The feel good answer may well be "yes" but is it the thoughtful and rational response? Our best and brightest minds throughout the first industrial revolution have brought us to our current situation, so do we reasonable expect drastically different results this next time around? Any delay in hammering out and implementing our best possible approach could even further jeopardize our chance for success.

An existing model of flourishing long-term industrial achievement would be exceedingly useful for us to emulate, but is such a prospect available? If we are able to set aside our hubris and intensify our perception and open-mindedness, an opportunity does exist for all business to emulate an amazingly successfully production system that has incorporated all the necessary strategies required for continuous prosperity. We will now turn our attention to a surprising source of invaluable guidance for every step of this reformation of business and society.

Guide Point 1: Our conventional approaches for producing goods and services routinely include unnecessarily insidious and tragic consequences for future generations of all life.

Chapter 2

Selecting a Design Consultant

A daunting challenge before us is the re-design of our commercial systems in a fashion that simultaneously provides profitable businesses and enhances the natural and human communities throughout time. Bringing such a bold set of intentions to fruition requires comprehensive, outside-the-box innovation and transports modern man into entirely uncharted waters. In the past, we have operated as if the earth held unlimited resources and a boundless capacity to absorb our potent array of debilitating pollutants. To this point, the focus of business endeavors has been overwhelmingly opportunistic with relatively short planning horizons that focus mostly on near-term financial gain. A sustainable business evolution involves a radical departure from conventionality and necessitates interdisciplinary challenges never previously considered.

A number of approaches in this book are outside traditional thought and, as yet, are not common topics of discussion around the proverbial water cooler. Recalling the earlier appeal for open-mindedness, you might find that our next point of discussion will push that request to its limit. I ask again that you seriously *consider* the next proposition, even if it is a bit uncomfortable to do so. If you do not initially accept the theme of the next section, perhaps you could file it in the "maybe" category for future consideration. Also do keep in mind that many movement supporters have found the following to be helpful and elucidating.

2.1 The Problem with Stewardship

The design task at hand would be less overwhelming if our efforts merely relied upon tweaking conventional business theory, adding to current bodies of knowledge, and using our collective human ingenuity. But that formula has been mankind's approach for advancement in the last several millennia. An examination of the overall results of our "business as usual approach" has exposed many serious systemic problems, and therefore, a reconsideration of certain core pivotal concepts is essential. Using the same basic premises and assumptions that have landed us in our current predicament would obviously prove unsuccessful. Our intentions of producing extraordinary results require us to use an extraordinary approach.

At this point, let us reconsider a key component of the Judeo-Christian ethic that is prevalent throughout Western society. Many Americans and Europeans believe man's proper environmental role is as a *wise steward* for all biota and regions of the natural world. Our superior intelligence and natural dominance, so the familiar ethic implies, places us in this position of control to skillfully supervise all planetary wild lands. Among other things, this ethic elevates humans above all other species and positions other life forms as part of a provisioning support structure for humanity. The idea of man as the superior and benevolent species wisely managing God's creation in respectful ways has indeed been embedded and reinforced in western society. The message in the Book of Genesis from the Old Testament seems quite clear: *God created the world in six days for humans* and rested on the seventh day.

Not surprisingly, Western environmentalists have adopted this theme of natural world stewardship as a basic tenet. This position offers an opportunity, perhaps even suggests a duty, for humans to take charge and decide the strategy to remedy the substantial global environmental degradation. This stewardship role has engaged many people, particularly in the past 100 years, in what is thought of as *enlightened management* of the natural world and no doubt involves many well-intentioned participants today. I suspect numerous readers of this book may subscribe to this belief.

This idea of human superiority, however, discourages the consideration of a very different kind of natural affiliation — *a kinship relationship — that involves a basic equality of all biota, including man.* Let us now overlay on this consideration some circumstances supported by a preponderance of scientific evidence. Science tells us that life on Earth has existed for at least 3.85 billion years and that modern man has existed only for the last 160,000 years. Project those numbers into the analogy of a mile-long period of life on Earth, and we see that man appeared only on the last half-inch of that mile-long stretch. Or, if we shrink the 3.85 billion year period down to a 365-day year beginning at midnight on 1st January, modern man appeared only on 31st December at 10:30pm. So, if all biota on Earth was put here for the expressed purpose of mankind's enjoyment and dominion, the guest of honor showing up at this year-long party on the last day at 90 minutes before midnight simply does not seem reasonable.

From the Eastern perspective, two major religions, Buddhism and Hinduism, have viewed for millennia man's stature and role as one of *kinship with* rather than *stewardship over* all other life. Today, nearly two billion members of these two religions alone are of the opinion that man has the same intrinsic value as all other sentient species. Let us now further consider the implications of this new kinship perspective in the context of a basic ideology currently shared by a large portion of world citizens.

Developing an appreciation and respect for the intrinsic value of other species and their role in the myriad of natural processes that foster life's abundance requires humility in the sense of recognizing man's true nature and role on Earth. Visionary Aldo Leopold, in the last chapter of his influential work, *A Sand County Almanac* published in 1947 shortly after his unexpected death, called for the next major refinement in our human code of ethics to acknowledge the basic existence rights of all natural world species. Leopold couched his "land ethic" among other previous moral code revisions such as equal rights for women and equality for people of all races. Even a preliminary acceptance of this kinship concept by Western thought paves the way for a profoundly useful opportunity in our re-design of commercial systems. If all other life on Earth is not ours to do with as we see fit, then we are bound by a different moral standard. If the human species does not possess a natural superiority and dominion over all other biota, then this circumstance allows humankind to assume the role of *student of nature* rather than master over the natural world. This new perspective opens up previously unconsidered but intriguing possibilities for provisioning ourselves. Let us now review humankind's situation and consider the application of this concept in the sustainable business movement.

2.2 Naturally Our Best Foot Forward

Man's legacy of environmental and social troubles across the globe stemming from past technological choices has been well-documented. Our predilection for fossil fuels, landfill-bound materials, natural resource exploitation, soil degradation, and persistent toxic waste is among the deepest failures. Considering our past performance, the expectation of our own cleverness to remedy our systemic industrial problems may not be in our best interests. Relying on our wit and ingenuity alone during the last few centuries has produced baleful long-term results, so expectations for a markedly different outcome of present-day industrial and social reform from a similar approach are simply not judicious.

A refreshingly ingenious alternative methodology has been suggested and popularized by biologist Janine Benyus in her ground-breaking 1997 book *Biomimicry — Innovation Inspired by Nature*. Benyus and other biomimics propose the idea that people emulate the genius of the natural world when growing our food, harnessing our energy, constructing things, conducting business, healing ourselves, processing information, and designing our communities. Benyus believes it is in our best interest to "quiet our cleverness" and explore the dominant industry on the planet — nature's industry — for reliable methods of provisioning our species. Benyus points out that the natural world has over 3.85 billion years of successful design experience in building durable and diverse life-supporting communities in a wide variety of environmental conditions. She notes that all other life on Earth takes a very different approach than do humans in regards to such necessities as energy, materials, food production, and community.

For most species, adapting to changing environmental conditions is accomplished by the occasional and random genetic changes in the cellular information of an organism. The acquisition of both genetically enabled physiological changes or genetically driven instinctive behavior can, in rare occasions, benefit subsequent generations of the organism. Humankind, on the other hand, has relied more heavily upon reflective behavior adaptations during most of our tenure to improve the chances of survival. The development of farming is an example of an enormously significant behavior adaptation of man. Agriculture emerged within human culture approximately 10,000 years ago and for the first time provided the means for groups of humans to acquire more food than was needed in the short term. Over time, increasingly dependable agricultural food surpluses provided the requisite accumulation of wealth that would enable distinctly different occupations to appear within groups of humans, and that made available the free time necessary to develop a variety of other cultural components such as religion, written language, mathematics, political systems, engineering, and trade relationships with other people. Other examples of significant human behavior adaptations include health care, manufacturing, and building design.

In the long term, however, our intellectual ability to organize complex social processes is ironically contributing to our undoing. Our legacy of technological change has established systems for living that produce quite different results from those systems used by all other biota. Historically, we have viewed our technology as a positive divergence from all other life and as an example of our species' unique superiority. A close examination of the insidious effects of our prolonged strategy reveals a corresponding steady decline of natural processes and services upon which all life, including man, depend. Fortunately, independent thinkers such as Benyus and others have recognized the critical opportunity to borrow from nature's wisdom and remodel our industry after the most thoroughly tested life-supporting processes in existence. The genius of the natural world has always been present for us to glean, and finally some of our contemporary designers have begun to take notice. Here are just a few examples of how designers have used nature to inspire our current products:

- Cockleburs and the fabric fastener Velcro®
- Abalone mother-of-pearl and high-tech ceramics
- Spider silk and stronger-than-steel cord
- Mussel shell adhesive and in-the-water ship hull repair
- Fish-shaped and decreased drag-coefficient vehicle design
- Toe-pads of geckos and strong, dry, and clean adhesives
- Porcupine quills and bird bones and structural design improvements

Benyus also identifies large-perspective applications of the genius of nature for a sustainable world. She suggests we model our cities after *Type III ecosystems* such as a redwood forest. Type III ecosystems typically reward diversity and interdependencies, build natural capital, procure locally, cycle all materials, and use the sun as their sole energy source.[6] Evidence suggests that these durable Type III natural communities have existed for many millions of years and provide an appropriate touchstone for the redesign of human communities around the world. This section indeed offers many controversial and exciting considerations and concepts to digest. The next few sections include even more nature-inspired systemic opportunities for sustainable business.

2.3 Pernicious Material Processes

Consider that nearly all your possessions will end up either in a landfill, a solid waste incinerator, or a junk yard. Some items will reach the end of the line in only a month; others will take years to arrive at their final destination. Clothes, furniture, appliances, vehicles, plastics, cardboard, and construction materials are part of our linear production systems (linear in the sense that materials are extracted, processed, sold, used for a period, and never used again). To make

---

[6] A commonly used term in this context is *recycle*, but this term is redundant. The term *cycle* is used hence throughout the book and refers to a continuous loop process and so stands alone without the *re*-prefix.

matters worse, our material preparation and refinement often yield substances that are used only once and *not designed for reprocessing* and that have *persistent toxins* mixed with benign natural materials. Persistent toxins are long-lasting, man-made, and not readily decomposed by natural processes. Unfortunately, many of these toxins eventually enter the human body through a variety of air, water, and food pathways and disrupt various body systems, cause cancer, and contribute to numerous other serious health problems.

Interior carpeting is an example of a commonly used product that is made of multiple persistent toxins. These contaminants fill the air inside our buildings via the wear and abrasion dust from foot traffic or from harmful vaporizing materials. Common nylon carpet pile material contains PBDE, a brominated fire retardant that damages the thyroid gland, the lymph system, and the nervous system. Benzene and p-Dichlorobenzene are known carcinogens contained in some carpeting pile. Carpet padding is commonly made of polyvinyl chloride and polyurethane, two other seriously toxic petrochemicals. Carpet adhesives such as 4-PC (4-phenylcyclohexene), styrene, ethyl benzene, and toluene add even more to the harmful mix routinely found in carpeted interiors. These persistent toxins tend to be most densely present in the air closest to the carpet: the exact locations of the particularly vulnerable toddlers in our homes.

Nature cannot afford such short-sighted and dangerous linear industrial processes. The natural world, powered by the sun, safely reuses all materials an endless number of times while using low-energy and low-temperature processes with no persistent toxic compounds. The natural world approach for material use is universal, durable, and effective. To illustrate this point, let us examine one of nature's most common industrial activities — the capture, storage, and use of energy.

2.4 Nature's Path of Production

The sugar–maple tree, common in the northeastern parts of the U.S., provides a good example of a natural production path for us to examine. A wide variety of benign chemical compounds are found in the leaf of a sugar–maple tree. During a summer day, the leaf captures a portion of the sun's energy that has traveled through space to Earth, while simultaneously reflecting the harmful ultraviolet portion of the solar energy spectrum back out into space. At the same time, tiny openings in the underside of the leaf called *stomata* take in carbon dioxide while a million root tips absorb and transport water up to the leaves for use in the process. During the night, the maple leaf turns its attention to converting this stored energy into incalculable chemical bonds of countless simple sugar molecules that become food for the tree. In the late fall, when the maple tree stops its sugar production because of cold weather and reduced daylight, the leaf falls to the ground, and eventually this former food factory is broken down by a variety of detritus organisms such as bacteria, fungi, and insect larva. Suspended in water and percolating through the soil, the dissolved materials gradually move downward, attaching and detaching from soil particles at various depths. During the time when these digested nutrients are in the root zone, root systems absorb and transport the valuable materials (formerly food factories) back into another plant where they will be used again, perhaps for leaf construction.

Natural processes such as these routinely cycle vital elements such as carbon, nitrogen, and phosphorous over and over again while using locally acquired energy from the sun and while producing no persistent harmful materials. Not only do they not produce harmful effects, they add tremendous value to their community: green plants discard the only significant source of molecular oxygen on Earth as sugar-production air emissions. Take a moment to think of the contribution of the Plant Kingdom to nature and our own lives. Three other familiar consequences of this energy-capturing natural technology described above are the taste of maple syrup on our pancakes, the beautiful grain and hue of maple furniture, and the glow of a fire from a maple log in our fireplaces.

Some early visionaries have already begun to tackle some of the core deficiencies in our industrial material strategies. In the early 1990s, German chemist Michael Braungart conceived what he calls the *Intelligent Product System*, which consists of only three categories of industrial products: consumables, durables, and unmarketables.[7]

---

[7] See Braungart and Elgelfried (1992) for a full explanation of this system.

Partnering with leading architect and designer William McDonough in the 2002 book *Cradle to Cradle*, he further refined this concept down to two product categories. The first type called consumables, or *products of consumption*, by definition would be made only of biodegradable materials. When products of consumption lose their usefulness, they would be broken down in their entirety by detritus organisms of the natural world and the resulting materials would be made available for use by other organisms. Examples of products that might fall into this category are packaging materials, shoes, and ink pens. The second type of product called durables, or *products of service*, would be made of materials toxic to living things such as heavy metal alloys and some petroleum-based compounds. Products of service would be durable goods routinely leased by the customer and owned by the producer, and when these products lose their usefulness, they would be returned to the manufacturer (closing the cycle), disassembled safely, and entirely re-processed into a new generation of products. Kitchen appliances, cell phones, most vehicle components, and personal computers would be examples of this type of product. Phased out would be the previously produced *unmarketables* (unusable toxins, such as nuclear waste) and *monstrous hybrids* (combined biodegradable and toxic compounds that now make up the vast majority of our manufactured goods) that fall into neither of the previous two categories. At current technology levels, these hybrids cannot be *cycled* or effectively reused, so they remain as bio-available poisons that time-release their contamination into the biosphere and into our bodies. Clearly, these materials are examples of poor quality design.

In this new materials protocol, sustainable manufacturers would classify each of their merchandise items as a product of service or a product of consumption. Decisions concerning which classification a product belonged in would be influenced by a number of factors such as the logistics of a possible take-back system, materials composition and abrasion demands, and life expectancy of the product. Let us apply this strategy to a common retail item — our clothing. Which of the two product types would make the most sense for apparel items?

As a product of consumption in this new paradigm, clothing would be made out of a variety of biodegradable materials, conditioners, and dyes. When the clothing items lose their usefulness, a trip to a composter for decomposition and the eventual return of the nutrients to our agricultural fields or gardens would fittingly close the biological cycle for these materials. In order to eliminate soil degradation, fossil-fuel pollution, synthetic pesticide and fertilizer pollution, and possible aquifer overdraft of conventional agriculture, the basic material used in our clothes (possibly cotton or hemp) would be grown via farming practices that use sustainable energy sources, enrich the soil fertility, and that employ local workers at a wage that allows them to support their families.

Let us now consider clothing items as products of service. In this scenario, clothing materials would be designed for use, reprocessing, and reuse for an indefinite number of times. With our considerable experience in crude oil-based synthetic textiles, the most expedient polymer-based raw material for apparel cloth would be petroleum; however, this choice carries some of the same environmental and social disadvantages presently associated with crude oil. Although thus far the on-the-customer performance of petroleum-based clothing items has exceeded bio-based materials, the more sensible and durable long-term raw material might be plant-based materials harvested from organic farming operations. Apparel companies implementing a product of service approach would also have to develop a convenient product return system that would transport worn-out clothing items back to the next-generation textile plants for reprocessing and reward customers for getting the outdated garment back to industry.

As this clothing example has implied, the initial product-type design decision for clothing producers requires considerable thought, planning, and trial and error. Fortunately, a number of apparel companies have already begun the process. The performance outdoor clothing company Patagonia, headquartered in Ventura, California, has taken the product of service approach with a line of clothing made from a polyester fabric called Capilene®. Patagonia now accepts any worn-out and laundered article made of Capilene® brought into any local Patagonia retail store or mailed to their service center in Reno, Nevada, U.S.A. The company then ships the worn-out clothing items to a plant in China on a cargo vessel that is normally near-empty (China imports relatively little from the U.S.) that re-polymerizes the crude oil-based material back into the Capilene® fabric, which is then used to make new garments for Patagonia. Patagonia is now poised for further progress in the movement by moving the overseas processing to a western state such as Nevada. This innovation, while significantly increasing its domestic cloth and garment manufacturing facilities, would demonstrate an even deeper commitment to the foundational principles of sustainable business. These efforts would establish additional regional operational connections (as in the natural world) and would keep additional monies and jobs located inside the U.S.

A second U.S.-based clothing company, Wickers, has decided to take the products of consumption approach in the design of a line of undergarments for men and women with a corn-based fabric called Ingeo™. Other forward-thinking manufacturers are producing lines of clothing using soybean oil, wood fiber, coconut oil, and bamboo. Organic cotton-based clothing items would fall into the product of consumption category as long as any dyes and fabric conditioners were also made only from biodegradable compounds. These intrepid companies are committing to these technologies in hopes of spear-heading a sustainable trend of apparel production. Does the product of service or product of consumption direction make more sense? Keep in mind that superior performance, durability, attractiveness, and affordability will accompany successful and intelligent product lines. Time will tell, but participants in the emerging sustainable clothing industry will most likely successfully employ both strategies, at least in the first few decades of the transition.

2.5 Two Closed-Loops into One

The previous two closed-loop clothing manufacturing strategies indeed take the lead from the natural world theme of continuously reusing all life-supporting materials. But a closer biomimicry-based consideration reveals that nature has no technical-nutrient cycle with persistent toxins as part of its materials production process. Sequestering persistent toxins inside a technical closed-loop process is quite different from nature's production system that uses only safe biodegradable materials for all of her material needs. So if our intention is to follow the universally healthy and dependable materials processes of nature, then part of our new production design plan would include the intentional and continual reduction of our products of service and the replacement of them whenever possible with intelligently designed products of consumption.

To illustrate this point, a single closed-loop electronic device that would conveniently serve all information and communication needs could take the place of a cell phone, MP3 player, vehicle sound system, home sound system, global positioning system, and even personal computer while drastically reducing the overall amount of closed-loop toxic compounds. A voice-operated multifunctional portable product providing all these compatible services and costing much less than the variety of devices previously required to deliver these separate services would provide better value for the customer, producer, natural world, and community. Today we have electronic products that are approaching this sort of comprehensive technology levels, and the complete version may be coming soon.

Another way to reduce the number of products of service might be the removal of ubiquitous items from this group, such as clothing, while transitioning to high-performance bio-based textiles produced in sustainable agricultural operations. Still another illustration might be a city that invests in a dependable, affordable, clean, comfortable, and safe mass transit system that reduces the number of vehicles (products of service) used by urban residents. The same city might have a visionary real estate company that works with city officials to rebuild residential neighborhoods with accompanying restaurants, retail stores, and recreation opportunities within walking distance, thereby further reducing the need for vehicles in the city.

Keeping toxins out of the biosphere requires the establishment of technical nutrient cycles for all existing products of service. These production cycles include the material-processing facilities, the manufacturing operations, the take-back systems, and the disassembly plants. Decreasing both the overall amount of toxins and the different types of dangerous materials inside technical nutrient cycles would be prudent for business, the natural world, and human communities. One direct benefit would be fewer overall toxins that require tracking and holding in closed-loop systems. Fewer industrial toxins mean less chances for these products of service materials to contaminate the environment where they could be ingested by organisms, including man, via food, water, or air. Another benefit of lowering the overall amount of technical materials would be a parallel reduction in hazardous working environments for industry employees who reprocess the noxious materials. Still another reduction advantage would be the elimination of selected closed-loop sequestration systems and corresponding expenses for some products that provide diminishing advantages over the product of consumption system. Lastly, there are the wisdom and yet unrecognized long-term rewards of mimicking the natural world's approach and the propensity for using only safe compounds in provisioning its current 10–15 million other species.

In her book *Living Downstream*, researcher and author Sandra Steingraber skillfully elucidates the widespread and disastrous effects upon human health by industrial processes, both past and present, that contain various types of *carcinogens* — cancer-causing compounds. Demonstrating critical-thinking skill and citing extensive credible research, Steingraber explains the effects of various carcinogens upon her own health and that of associates and friends. Steingraber skillfully discusses the undeniable human misery and financial loss that are spawned by the indiscriminate use of our wide range of industrial toxins. This common practice is a needless tragedy that continues to deteriorate and shorten the productive lives of incalculable innocent adults, adolescents, and children. In fact, if all the externalized costs of carcinogenic pollutants, such as time off from work and hospitalization costs, were actually paid by the people who received the beneficial part of the toxic production process (in other words, a situation approaching a free-market system), these particularly injurious practices would be priced out of business. And this accounting change still has not attempted to assign a value for the accompanying human misery of suffering from cancer or the loss of a loved one from this disease.

When compared to our current cradle-to-grave materials system, segregating technical toxic stock and biodegradable materials would deliver major advantages throughout time for business and communities. This new manufacturing approach would substantially reduce toxic substances in the biosphere, lessen the amount of virgin materials extracted and energy needed to power the process, establish a return system for nutrients back to our agricultural soils, and lower raw-material costs for manufacturers. Not limited to manufacturing, biomimicry-based innovation is available to all business types for numerous improvements in material use and information flows. Still another immense opportunity to benefit from nature's wisdom lies in our energy strategies for transportation, commercial operations, and residential needs. Let us now consider an intelligent, nature-inspired approach to energy production for our industrial, retail, and residential world.

2.6 Nature's Energy Path

Most developed nations still primarily rely upon fossil fuels to meet both transportation and stationary energy needs. We extract, transport, process, and burn inordinate amounts of crude oil, natural gas, and coal each day in the U.S. alone. In addition to providing the energy that powers our industrial and personal endeavors, dependency upon fossil fuels also costs the U.S. dearly in terms of trade deficit, international military actions, human health problems, and climate change. Clearly, Earth's major ecosystems have a much preferred energy legacy. Let us take a look at how the natural world meets its energy needs and consider other possible applications of nature's wisdom for humankind.

Nature has been remarkably single-minded in her procurement of energy for all of life's activities. Despite the almost incomprehensible diversity of biota on this planet, life depends upon an independent nuclear fusion power plant located 93 million miles away for all energy needs. This power plant has been operating for about five and a half billion years and is expected to last another five or six billion years. This boundless source of energy requires no up-front construction cost, no maintenance, and does not deposit pollution in the air, water, or soil. The vast distance separating the earth from the sun protects us from minor malfunctions and irregularities. Countless billions of these power plants exist in the universe. Besides providing a free source of energy for billions of years, these stars are also responsible for the synthesis and distribution of all the known elements of the cosmos. The atoms of this book that you are reading were previously forged inside a star somewhere in the cosmos. Our natural world is so smitten by this energy source that it has evolved completely dependent upon the sun for all energy needs — without a back-up source or secondary power supply. Any species that might have deviated from this strategy is simply not in existence any longer.

How has nature's single-source energy gamble paid off? Life on Earth has thrived for extended periods of the last 3.85 billion years. Today, millions of different species populate a wide variety of solar-powered natural communities in the oceans, high alpine valleys, equatorial rainforests, hot and cold deserts, and polar tundra. Green plants are the foundation of Earth's rich biodiversity as they routinely capture, store, and pass along the sun's energy to all other living things. Interestingly, energy does not continually cycle in the natural world as materials do; rather, the *constant daytime input of sunlight* powers the diverse and rich ecosystems. The sun's energy is stored and then passed along from life form to life form, and it is eventually dissipated as heat, a little at a time, at each life level.

During its long tenure, life has tenaciously survived a number of catastrophic global environmental events. Considerable scientific evidence suggests that one such occurrence approximately 250 million years ago extirpated up to 95% of existing species — but life continued. Another cataclysm almost 65 million years ago caused an estimated 75% of all species to disappear. Today, between 10 and 15 million species are estimated to exist and to continue this resilient legacy of diverse, interdependent, sun-powered fecundity. Solar energy is affirmed in the flight of birds, in our woodstove fires, in the force of hurricanes, and even in the taste of a cheeseburger.

2.7   Following Nature's Energy Path

The continuous success of solar-powered life throughout the ages provides a reliable and durable energy design model for sustainable business. If we follow nature's lead, this free, local, abundant, and clean energy source will in time replace our current problem-ridden energy choices as a value-laden alternative. Community-procured solar energy for transportation, industrial, and residential needs would provide stable local employment and would dramatically reduce the dollars leaving cities for distant energy sources and thereby build wealth inside local economies. Electricity, cleanly generated and used inside each of our communities, offers additional advantages such as reduced transmission-line infrastructure and maintenance costs, less energy consumed in moving electricity from a regional power plant to the consumer, and reduced vulnerability of power-supply to malfunction or sabotage.

Today, many environmentally conscious energy specialists recommend a power distribution system based on a variety of alternative production schemes available from the existing opportunities within a region. Typical scenarios often include a combination of solid waste and biofuels combustion, hydroelectricity, and "clean" coal technology. This multi-source energy strategy may reduce harmful local effects, particularly in the short term, but it also contains significant conceptual long-term liabilities that degrade living conditions in distant locations. Consider all the consequences from each of these alternative energy sources listed above.

Waste-to-energy plants burn solid municipal waste to generate electricity, perpetuate the concept of waste, emit dangerous industrial air pollutants, produce concentrated toxic ash and encourage linear manufacturing systems and natural resource exploitation. Biofuel production primarily relies upon fossil-fuel powered mechanized agriculture, which continues to degrade soils, put pesticides into our drinking water, decrease food production, and add carbon dioxide (a greenhouse gas) to the atmosphere. Few new hydroelectric dam sites exist in the U.S. today; and existing dams destroy irreplaceable riparian habitat, flood fertile bottomland farmland, and obstruct the migration patterns of certain species of fish, including salmon and steelhead. Finally, "clean" coal technology is a misnomer: it is expensive, it only slightly reduces overall pollution, and it concentrates the toxicity and moves pollution from one waste stream (air) to another (solids).

If we are to follow nature's lead and convert to a strategy that would provide our energy needs for millennia to come without negative side effects, solar energy will be the centerpiece of our energy technology. Nature has ingeniously used solar power for all biotic activities in polar latitudes as well as in cloud-dominated temperate regions of the world. A global commitment to solar technology will provide our species with available and abundant local energy for another five billion years with little danger of supply interruption, significant pollution, or climate-changing side effects. Intelligent systems that capture energy from the sun to power our businesses, transportation, and homes will provide lasting and rewarding employment worldwide and will prove well worth the changeover investment in time and resources. Consider the long-term employment and economic boost from locally capturing, storing, and distributing all the energy needs of your community. Imagine a city with the outsides of all buildings made of windows, vegetative material, or photovoltaic (PV) surfaces (generating electricity from sunlight) that generate both the stationary and personal vehicle energy needs of the occupants. The latitude location and the number of sunny days per year will initially determine the need for additional power sources, but constantly improving technological efficiency of PV systems and the mechanical efficiency of all power-driven devices will continually lower the cost of energy and raise the percentage of energy provided by the sun.

2.8 Other Sun-Powered Opportunities

The fusion nuclear reactor 93 million miles away gives us some additional opportunities for harnessing indirect solar energy in the form of wind, wave, and tidal forces at numerous locations around the globe. Our global wind patterns are powered by the sun's differential heating of the atmospheric gasses with coastal locations and interior flatlands generally providing the best prospects to harvest a reasonably strong and consistent wind supply. However, the intermittent and tumultuous nature of wind proves particularly challenging for designers of durable and efficient wind-power-generating equipment. Wind turbines are quite noticeable on the landscape or shoreline and can pose an aesthetic drawback to some communities. Nevertheless, using the wind to generate electricity satisfies the definition of sustainable energy — a technology that can meet our energy needs indefinitely without negative effects — and can provide the total power production for some wind-rich regions.

Generating electricity from ocean waves and tidal forces also brings us some advantages and disadvantages. On the plus side, energy from the ocean offers densely populated coastal areas the opportunity to harness very large amounts of sustainable energy at the very location where it is needed by large numbers of people. On the negative side, quite a few technological challenges remain to be solved before this energy choice is available to power large metropolitan groups. Fortunately, no matter which combination of sustainable energy choices a region selects, other design improvements currently underway such as intelligent building design, improved mechanical efficiency, and resident-friendly community design, will lower the per person demand for energy and will help the transition to durable, healthy, and locally run energy supplies.

2.9 Envision a Sun-Powered Human Society

A fully transitioned sun-powered U.S. economy will offer quite a contrast from the fossil fuel and nuclear-powered economic engines of today. Moving toward this nature-inspired ideal will require a sizeable national investment and several decades of infrastructure changeover, but the upside payoff implications are enormous. Gone will be the insidiously injurious air, water, and soil pollution from the extraction, transportation, processing, and combustion of fossil fuels. Our single nuclear power plant will be a safe 93 million miles away, along with all the dangerous accompanying radioactive materials. As the demand for crude oil, coal, and natural gas continually shrinks, greenhouse gas emissions will correspondingly decrease, and our atmosphere will begin to self-regulate its constituency again. Part of the climate change recovery process will no doubt include massive carbon sequestration efforts from worldwide reforestation programs and site-appropriate solar technology transfers to communities inside developing nations. As we begin to recognize that a sustainable world requires the well-being of all members of all species (including humans), international political relationships will also purposefully evolve and deepen.

As the energy transformation continues around the world, the corresponding decrease in crude oil demand will dissolve any remnant of the previously influential Organization of Petroleum Exporting Countries (OPEC). "The Age of Fossil Fuels" section in future world history books will be relatively brief with the period comprising less than 400 years. Major oil companies, the economic juggernauts of conventional energy, have the means to follow the early lead of global energy corporations such as British Petroleum (BP) and begin to diversify their operations to small-scale solar-powered energy production systems; these systems would deliver hydrogen from the process of "*clean hydrolysis*" (the passing of a sustainably generated electric current through water, yielding hydrogen and oxygen) that would be used to supply stationary and vehicle fuel cells and for hydrogen combustion turbines in a variety of regional markets. Rather than resisting the conversion to clean energy, these cash-flush oil corporations have the opportunity to position themselves as early change agents for an intelligent energy infrastructure. If major oil companies do indeed reorganize and become sustainable energy-providers, the metamorphosis will require considerable effort and capital investment but will prove to be advantageous for their businesses in the long term.

Opportunities also exist to research, develop, and market a plethora of plant-based materials that will replace petrochemicals in many manufacturing applications. Actually, this opportunity will be a resumption of an earlier research emphasis in this field that was begun in the pre-World War II years. These plant-based production materials will be part of the products of consumption side of the materials equation. Some high-performance petroleum-based polymers will also be used initially for various components in the durable products of service cycle. Forward thinking diversified energy companies will continue to meet the shrinking petroleum demand but will derive an ever-growing majority of revenues from the expanding demand for clean and healthy energy and material systems.

2.10 Cutting Our Nuclear Power Losses

A broad-based commercial and residential commitment to the continued refinement of solar, wind, geothermal, and ocean power technology to generate electricity will help dissolve the lingering consideration for either commissioning new commercial nuclear power plants or refurbishing worn-out units. Current high consumer demand for electrical power can be mitigated by significant mechanical efficiency improvements in all sectors of the market. The savings in electric bills from a lowered demand can help finance the research and development needed for further efficiency gains. Even at current PV and wind-power technology levels, and disregarding the serious and long-lasting public safety issues of high-level nuclear waste, the high cost of nuclear power production has effectively priced itself out of the western energy market. Further advances in PV and wind technology will provide even more economic, environmental, and social incentives for sun-powered sources of energy. Some state governments are furthering this effort by adapting aggressive energy portfolio standards that target a specific percentage of commercial energy to be generated by renewable sources, which does include solar and wind power.

Unfortunately, our 50-year ill-advised history of commercial nuclear power now requires a $70 billion-plus consumer outlay for high-level nuclear waste transportation and storage from our 110 commercial nuclear power plants to the permanent storage facility at Yucca Mountain, Nevada. At least four generations of Americans must also assume the considerable risk involved in moving the thousands of tons of this waste across the nation over the next 75 years. And after this monumental logistical task is completed, hundreds of future generations of U.S. citizens must monitor and guard the persistently dangerous radioactive material for tens of thousands of years.

Commercial nuclear power plants have always been a bad idea, particularly considering the risk and life-cycle costs that are passed on to posterity. The argument that continued investment in nuclear power is now a necessary part of a global warming avoidance strategy is also flawed and shortsighted. This approach would only reduce greenhouse gas emissions at the expense of transferring a large portion of the cost of nuclear power, and the vulnerability to terrorism, sabotage, and accidents, to future generations. Transportation and storage costs for the high-level nuclear waste, along with the inevitable decommissioning costs of the power plants themselves, are causing the nuclear power industry to collapse under its own weight. Citizens throughout time are much better served by moving away from commercial nuclear power and fossil fuels and turning to a safe, abundant, clean, durable, and reliable energy strategy to meet energy needs. Our only affordable and safe nuclear reactor is the Sun, and its continuous fusion reaction provides more than ample opportunity to meet the energy needs for all the millions of species on Earth for the next few billion years without perpetual risk and exorbitant expense.

2.11 The Advantages of Local Energy Production

Another valuable energy lesson the natural world offers us involves the theme of *locally captured and distributed energy*. As noted earlier, all life on Earth is made possible by green plants capturing and storing a small portion of *local* incoming solar energy in the form of simple sugars. This chemical energy is eventually passed on to all other biota along food webs that end with the detritus feeders consuming the dead plant and animal materials and their waste products. Although the preponderance of natural world energy is procured and distributed locally, this local power concept has not been mirrored in our developed world. On the contrary, large centralized commercial power plants rely on coal, natural gas, and enriched uranium from distant sources and utilities maintain expansive and expensive electrical grid distribution systems that supply millions of scattered industrial, commercial, and residential customers throughout the developed world. The state of the antiquated U.S. electrical grid system is poor, as illustrated by the series of regional brown outs and complete power failures experienced in the last decade. Transitioning to locally distributed power production makes much more sense in the long-run when compared with efforts to maintain a design-flawed and outdated centralized power infrastructure.

Nature, as our design consultant, endorses solar-based power that is locally procured in communities such as in the splendid redwood groves of California's Sierra Nevada Mountains, the oak/hickory forests of Southern Illinois, or the short-grass prairies of the Great Plains Region. A de-centralized energy approach will use a localized workforce to build, maintain, and operate the numerous small community power stations and eliminate our vulnerability to regional power failures and volatile fuel prices. This long-term strategy makes sense for all stakeholders except those commercial power companies that would stubbornly resist the transition to smaller, locally controlled power producers.

Typically a single pearl of nature's wisdom provides goodness on many levels, solves a variety of problems, and provides value for our expanded concept of community. An indication of durable and intelligent innovation is a win-win-win situation for all members of our community — a concept that is increasingly recognized by leaders of sustainable business. Clearly, de-centralized and locally operated direct and indirect solar energy systems provide this sort of multiple-value production and offer us a positive and rewarding energy legacy to pass on to future generations.

2.12 Changing Energy Trends

The changeover to decentralized, small-scale solar or wind power production is certainly a formidable economic challenge but the conversion has already begun. The fastest growing energy sector in the world is now solar and wind technology, with many mainstream large organizations such as FedEx, Timberline, Sony, PepsiCo, Wal-Mart, Honda, and the U.S. Army having begun to invest in wind and solar energy. Today, in the southwestern U.S., nine commercial solar power plants produce about 350 megawatts of electricity capable of powering more than 85,500 homes, and many more such operations are on the horizon. The Department of Energy's *Million Solar Roofs* program kicked off in 1998 and is on schedule to promote *one million solar energy systems* installed on rooftops across the United States by 2010. Cities such as Oakland, Sacramento, San Jose, San Francisco, San Diego, Portland (Oregon), Boston, and Austin currently lead the U.S. in terms of the percentage of energy generated from renewable sources.

From a global perspective, German and Japan combined to generate over 80% of solar-generated electricity worldwide in 2006. Today, Germany operates 15 of the world's 20 largest photovoltaic power facilities and is adding even more capacity, although it experiences less than half the sunny days as the southwestern U.S. Over 40,000 Germans are employed in manufacturing photovoltaic panels and other solar equipment, and another 15,000 work for companies that make solar heating systems for homes and businesses. Total global sales for solar equipment topped $9.5 billion in 2006, and this amount is growing at a 20% annual rate with a staggering upside.[8]

In 2006, four BP solar-energy-component production sites located in Spain, India, Australia, and the U.S. produced PV equipment capable of generating 180 megawatts of energy (1 megawatt = 1 million watts; a compact fluorescent light needed at night to read this book uses about 25 watts of electricity). One of the leading manufacturers of the newly developed thin film PV technology is United Solar Ovonic LLC with three manufacturing facilities in Michigan and a fourth in Mexico with a workforce of over 1,000 employees. The flexible, polycrystalline thin film PV material adheres to plastic, glass, and stainless steel in nearly any shape and size and has increased the variety of application possibilities for self-supporting energy production.

Considerable progress has also been made in the design of wind turbines with newer models proving more durable and generating more electricity at lower wind speeds. UPC Wind is one of the leading U.S. wind-power companies and (in 2006) was developing over

---

[8] See Reguly (2008) for an in-depth treatment of European energy trends.

3,000 megawatts of wind-power projects. Clipper Windpower Inc., headquartered near Santa Barbara, CA, is an example of a rapidly growing company that both produces wind turbines and develops wind-power-generating projects in the U.S. and Europe. In addition to larger commercial-sized wind-power units, smaller turbines are now available from a number of domestic sources and are sized for single- or multiple-family homes and small or medium-sized businesses that are located in areas of sufficient wind supply.

Even at current technology levels, small-scale, locally owned solar and wind power stations offer dependable and affordable electricity to residential and commercial consumers as well as a durable employment sector with virtually no undesirable effects on natural or human communities throughout time. Clean and renewable power for our businesses and homes sets the stage for efficiency improvements not for the purpose of reducing pollution, but rather, for providing opportunities for energy-production systems that are small, affordable, and self-sufficient. By embedding another vital economic sector back into local economies, our energy dollars will now help revitalize and perpetually support our communities.

A similar approach to transportation reform has potential for corresponding improvements. Consider the prospects of product of service vehicles equipped with highly efficient electric motors powered either by a bank of high-tech batteries charged with wind/solar-produced electricity or from a stack of fuel cells that use oxygen from the air and hydrogen from wind/solar-powered electrolysis. In the not-too-distant future, look for quiet, quick, battery-powered electric vehicles capable of traveling 300-plus miles between recharging to compete with and eventually replace the combustion engine and the gasoline/electric hybrid vehicle.

Author and visionary Paul Hawken suggests that in addition to providing clean and reliable transportation, private fuel-cell vehicles would have the capability to power our homes and to provide electricity to our employers.[9] Gasoline/electric hybrid vehicles such as the Toyota Prius have already begun a transportation technology

---

[9] See Hawken, *et al.* (1999) for further discussion on personal energy systems.

changeover, but significant barriers must still be overcome in order for hydrogen to replace crude oil as our effective energy carrier for transportation. Clean hydrogen production facilities, a reliable national distribution system, and improved hydrogen storage technology are major challenges that remain. Nevertheless, further research and development in this regard would add another quality piece to the sustainable business puzzle.

2.13 Innovations Solving Multiple Problems

A creative, practical, and durable energy strategy, when combined with other civic amenities such as walkable urban landscapes and an assortment of locally owned businesses, provide a solid foundation for prosperous and enjoyable communities. As business recognizes the advantages of using *locally available* resources and develops collaborative *local business relationships*, we indeed mimic the interdependency theme of natural ecosystems. Although a durable and healthy local economy does provide a solid economic base, sustainable communities need not restrict themselves to solely local business relationships; indeed, when only certain natural resources are available in other regions, functioning trade relationships are prudent. Just as we might breathe air produced by the Amazon rainforest and the same rainforest might use the carbon dioxide from our exhalation, so will distant human communities complement each other's endeavors.

For example, consider the uniquely beautiful Southwest Region of the U.S. with its variety of quaint and comfortable canyonland resorts. Imagine these locally owned establishments patronized by vacationing Midwestern residents, some of whom sustainably harvest and process their indigenous hardwoods into a variety of beautiful and durable furniture items available for purchase by the innkeepers. Neither the scenery nor the hardwood is available in both regions, and so a trade relationship in tourism and furniture makes both regions more prosperous and stable.

The wisdom of developing diverse and interdependent communities that primarily use locally available resources has been a common formula throughout the ages for mature ecosystems around the world. The following chapters introduce other innovations inspired by nature, and in nearly each case, natural systems have been used to gauge the appropriateness of the change under consideration. Natural processes and individual species have adjusted to the changing set of environmental conditions for millions of years, and today's rich diversity of life is the result of the unending series of life's adaptation to change. Recognizing the opportunity for man to emulate these durable natural themes eliminates the need for us to sculpt sustainable production systems in isolation. Together we can cultivate an attitude of humility, an open mind, a meticulous inquisition of nature, and an unrelenting determination to transform our energy and material production and consumption patterns into brilliant reflections of natural world systems.

Guide Point 2: A small but widespread group of visionaries has begun a redesign of business that provides profitable and stable companies, durable and vibrant human communities, and a healthy and diverse natural environment. The design criterion for this process is to mimic natural world energy and materials themes.

Chapter 3

The Bull's Eye

Previously, a number of sobering environmental and social problems were outlined that are direct results of short-sighted technological expansions. Rather than relying on government to orchestrate a solution, a small but determined collection of entrepreneurs from various business sectors and locations have begun to re-envision and re-invent our global industrial system. Their new approach offers businesses improved long-term financial stability and a positive relationship with the natural world and human communities. The enduring rewards from using proven natural world production themes as models for business are becoming increasingly clear. At this point, for some, it may seem foolish for business leaders *not* to take advantage of the innumerable trial-and-error experiences of life on Earth and to make use of the lessons learned in the redesign of our commercial endeavors. For you, the reader, recognizing, respecting, and using natural themes in this commercial revolution has hopefully begun to seem rational, sensible, and even essential.

3.1 The Triple Top-Line

After considering the various negative consequences of conventional business, you may be in favor of major changes but at the same time be somewhat unsure about the most appropriate actions for your organization. A conceptual tool available to assist with these considerations is called the *triple top-line, or* TTL (also referred to as the *triple bottom-line* but using the term "bottom-line" may give the impression that something negative or inferior is involved when the contrary is true).[10] The TTL establishes three *simultaneous*

---

[10] See Elkington (1994) for the source of the triple bottom-line term.

requirements of all sustainable business innovation — financial benefits for the company, natural world benefits, and social benefits for employees and members of the local community — with each of these three components enjoying equal status. The reasoning behind this conceptual design by early organizers is that each part of the TTL is inextricably tied to the other two, and only commercial activity that equally supports all three components will have the capacity to continue indefinitely and aid in the transition into a *sustainable business.*

Consider, for example, a decision by the board of directors of Metro Health Hospital in Grand Rapids, Michigan to include a large vegetative roof (or green roof) over the administrative office portion of their newly constructed hospital complex in 2007. Vegetated roofs include some form of soil medium and herbaceous plants that grow and cover the roof surface. Metro's one-plus-acre green roof is in full view of most patient rooms and is considerably more pleasing than a traditional dark, flat tarred roof with various noisy mechanical units (air conditioners, for example) and unattractive vent pipes. Hospital administrators were convinced that non-critical patients will recover faster and be more relaxed in their surroundings during their stay when provided with this aesthetically pleasing view of nature.

Vegetative roofs also produce oxygen, reduce storm water runoff, and provide a habitat for certain species of birds and insects. Properly constructed green roofs are more durable than conventional roofs in large part because the foliage reflects nearly all of the ultraviolet radiation back to space before it can deteriorate deeper roofing materials. Green roofs also provide additional thermal and noise insulation for the floors beneath them, keeping the interior warmer in the winter, cooler in the summer, and quieter all year round.

From a TTL perspective, Metro's green roof reduces utility bills, enhances the natural environment with oxygen-producing killdeer nesting habitat, and provides patients with a more pleasing setting in which to recuperate. Administrators at Metro Health Hospital recognized that the green roof would provide a *competitive advantage* for their health care facility when compared to a conventional flat roof.

Metro has hit the bull's eye of TTL sustainable business innovation, as this one innovation continually provides financial, environmental, and social value over time. The payback period for this investment not only makes sense from a financial perspective but also from the two other components of sustainable business — nature and the human community.

3.2 The Short Post on the Three-Legged Stool

In practice, the most often discounted or ignored component of the TTL is the element of social benefits. For years, environmental sentiment has engendered *green business practices*, mostly in the form of efficiency improvements that lowered production costs and modestly reduced the environmental burden. The overriding goal of conventional business has always been to increase profits and market share, often by lowering production costs, and the business relevance of improving relationships with employees and nearby communities is often counter-intuitive in the U.S.

On the other side of the world, Japan built an enormously productive industrial empire after World War II within a culture where supervisors routinely pressure workers for increased productivity without providing the incentives of a better working environment or higher compensation levels. Today in Japanese culture, quitting one company and going to work for another is generally considered dishonorable and the social pressure to stay with your current employer is strong, no matter how unfair the treatment. Not surprisingly, the social component of the triple top-line is even stranger to Japanese than to U.S. business leaders. Incidentally, the per capita suicide rate among the Japanese workforce is one of the highest in the developed world.

In the West, an increasing number of savvy entrepreneurs are recognizing that investing in a comfortable, healthy, and supportive employee work environment pays large and lasting dividends. For example, a single mother employee who places her infant in her worksite day-care center (as opposed to one that is across town) will worry less about her child during working hours, particularly if she is able to visit her youngster during her lunch hour and break periods. If this employee has a comfortable work-station with amenities such as constant fresh air and ambient outdoor light, along with the opportunity to influence procedural changes that will enhance her job performance, she will likely be much more creative, productive, and loyal to her company. Human resource directors are keenly aware of the expense involved in attracting, training, and retaining valuable workers. After committing such a sizeable financial investment to its workforce, decision makers are wise to provide a setting that will promote contented and productive employees. In addition to the financial rewards for business, investing in employee welfare is magnanimous and ethical.

3.3 The Nature of the Movement

Meaningful progress toward a vigorous and durable industrial system will be marked by business *routinely* crafting and implementing TTL improvements. Similarly, a refocused business culture will encourage *related systems thinking and innovation*; groups of employees operating in such a culture will put TTL ideas into practice, assess the results, and continually find creative ways to increase profits, enhance the natural environment, and support each other and their community. Sustainable business design takes into account *all the side effects* of delivering their products and services, including any natural resource extraction, processing, facility operations, administration, and similar supply-chain considerations. In order to assess and continuously improve all the resulting effects of a particular good or service through time, engaged managers use this broad-based approach called *life-cycle analysis* as a regular tool for innovation.

This bourgeoning sustainable business movement is already thriving in a variety of business sectors including agriculture, architecture, health care, food service, retail, government, higher education, and various manufacturing applications. Unlike other cultural movements in history, this revolution has its origins in a variety of times, locations, and independent participants primarily throughout the Americas and Europe. Unnamed for much of its beginnings, the movement term that has taken hold is "*sustainable business*," although a more representative title certainly seems appropriate. The essence of *sustainable* in this context is *the capacity to continue indefinitely*, but the upside of the movement provides much more to business than simply a recipe for survival. Inherent in this new conception of business is a requisite essence that is benevolent, nourishing, and supportive for all life on Earth for all time. Rather than moving toward a trend of restraint and inhibition, qualities such as beauty, richness, and splendor can be expected as endemic characteristics in both human and natural communities. Perhaps as the movement matures, a more fitting moniker such as *bountiful business* or simply *intelligent business* might evolve into the language of the movement.

Applying the term *sustainable* to individual businesses is a misnomer. At best, single establishments, companies, or even cities can position themselves only as a positive constituent within a *global scale system* of sustainability on planet Earth, which requires both a healthy natural world and a healthy global human community that provides *opportunity* to flourish for all inhabitants for all time. The unadulterated and deeper meaning of our chosen term *sustainable* includes this imperative of *global interconnectedness* and the recognition that the tenure of all living things is inextricably embedded in the fate of all others. This characteristic of global-scale interdependency for all life has been commonly missing in open discussions of sustainability. To use a familiar analogy, the chain of *sustainability* is only as strong as its weakest link, and business, the human community, and the natural world represent vital links for a sustainable world. Business and commerce certainly have the lion's share to accomplish in order for a sustainable world to become a reality; the content of this book is focused on that particular challenge, and we will further explore the ramifications of the interdependencies of sustainable business in subsequent pages. SB requires global interconnectedness view that positions individual businesses as parts of the sustainable world, not sustainable themselves.

3.4 High Stakes and New Takes

As we incrementally eliminate the concept of waste and pollution, and join all other life on Earth in solar-powered, closed-loop material

As we continue to let nature support us it will be easier for us to support nature.

50   *Fundamentals of Sustainable Business*

cycles that are engaged by a well-supported labor force, a more vigorous set of nature-based human systems will produce a corresponding increase in vitally important ecological services. Perhaps the most critically compromised of all services — climate stabilization — will return to near "normal" conditions and enable Earth to resume its natural climate change process. However, this outcome is far from certain; the climate change process may already be irretrievably altered. Only time will tell if a prolonged period of warmer global temperatures and corresponding changes in precipitation patterns are on the near horizon or, alternately, if we have set in motion the atmospheric triggers that will soon move Earth into another ice age. Our climate models include both scenarios as possibilities, and hopefully the concerted human response will be timely and sufficient to minimize the somber repercussions for all life on Earth. If our response is too late or inadequate, a new set of climatic conditions may lower Earth's human carrying capacity as well as change geographical locations that are most conducive to human habitation.

The ramifications of a robust global sustainability movement suggest that citizens will come to value a strong *sense of place* within their communities and to value strong TTL innovations that improve the quality of life for all. One interesting result of movement maturation for our cityscapes will be the obsolescence of zoning as TTL-pursuing business will assume a much more supportive character toward urban residents. Children will play safely in beautiful areas adjacent to our handsome production facilities without the danger of toxins in the soil, air, or water. A quiet, clean, convenient, and affordable transportation system will be the rule, with intelligently renovated walkable communities dominating the global urban landscape. A much larger portion of our food will be grown within, and immediately adjacent to, urban areas. Numerous urban greenhouse operations will routinely use secondary heat from a variety of industrial and residential sources, thereby significantly extending the growing season of cooler localities, reducing their dependency on distant food products, and further contributing toward full and rewarding community employment.

The need for garbage trucks and solid waste haulers will nearly disappear as the concept of material waste is eliminated. Effective, efficient, and durable delivery schemes will move products of service back to reprocessing plants and products of consumption back to the soil. In this emerging economy, a variety of service sector opportunities will be filled by a growing number of locally owned businesses that routinely engage in TTL-guided operations. Community members will provide a large part of their own food, merchandise, and basic services. After recognizing the long-term advantages of a strong manufacturing sector, these operations will move back from off-shore to local communities. The phasing out of fugitive industrial toxins will significantly lower the incidence of cancer and other pollution-related diseases. The health care industry will concentrate on a myriad of preventive services and promote healthy lifestyles. It is possible that we will have a system in place where doctors have a compelling incentive to encourage healthy lifestyles because their compensation will be partially based on how long a client is healthy rather than only on treatment services provided for sick patients. Hopefully, these examples provide insight into sizeable rewards from the systemic modifications we might expect as a result of our shifting to an intelligent and delightful system of business within numerous sustainable communities. Chapter 7 takes you on an extensive time-traveling adventure to a sustainable community of the future, but this segment offers a taste of such kinship for now.

3.5 How Do We Begin?

Up to this point, we have concentrated on investigating specific characteristics of sustainable business and vibrant communities, and from a pragmatic viewpoint, some of these goals may seem beyond the reach of society. We have outlined where we want to go, but the specifics of "How do we get there?" may be less clear. For the new energy and material sectors, the transformation intuitively requires an immense amount of research, time, and resources. What are the steps businesses will take as they undergo a metamorphosis into this fresh brand of TTL-based activities? These are reasonable questions, and to answer them, we turn to the concept of *transition strategies for sustainable business*, as well as some of the common misconceptions and some of the pitfalls that accompany this tenuous transition phase.

A definitive and clear initial set of declared intentions for human-kind in the sustainable business movement is critical for the success we have outlined. We have moved beyond simply reducing our day-to-day damages upon the natural world and ourselves; rather, part of our goal is to make all industrial activity at its least, benign to all living systems, and at its most, nourishing and supportive of the world community. We endeavor to accomplish this goal not by assuming additional costs for business but instead by increasing profits, particularly in the long run. Pioneers of this movement assume the challenge of providing participating businesses a *competitive advantage* over conventional business practices throughout the transition process. In fact, many believe that the defining principles of sustainable business will be indispensable for successful businesses in the future.

After establishing biomimicry-guided ambitions for their companies, sustainable business advocates are ready to begin the deliberate process of TTL innovation. As a general rule, this transition is most successful in organizations with leaders who passionately champion the movement and who provide their lieutenants with a foundational expertise in sustainable business through a variety of on- and off-site educational sessions. These informed department managers then typically share this new competency with their associates and thereby sponsor a basic understanding of sustainable business throughout the organization.

At this point, most engaged employees have acquired a basic appreciation of the natural world and its processes, the adverse effects of most conventional industrial practices, the TTL concept, and various other tenets of the movement. This fast-track education emphasis enables all employees to talk the same sustainability language and to act in a concerted way to bring about this newly defined mission of the institution. Often this incremental process is referred to as *a change in the organizational culture of a business* and is vital for a successful transition toward sustainable business.

Change agents, those employees inside organizations that have been particularly inspired by the movement, are now ready to develop internal processes involving all departments and employee levels that generate TTL outcomes. Executives and managers encourage and incentivize the submission of effective innovation proposals by all personnel and include such projects in routine job responsibilities. Broad-based in-house committees are formed that review TTL proposals, solicit input from the staff who will be most affected by the proposal, and work with idea-submitters to improve the proposed innovation. The refined TTL proposals are then forwarded to decision-makers and, upon their approval and funding, are implemented within the organization. Innovations typically involve nearly every facet of an organization with a common theme of making the organization simultaneously more profitable and a better member of both the natural and human communities.

[handwritten notes: 1. clear declared intentions. 5. develop internal processes for TTL. 6. Review committees set up for the innovs. 7. TTL implementations. — nourishing ind... aa kinds. 2. Increase profits w/ competitive adv. 3. Biomimicry + TTL training. 4. Change in culture.]

3.6 No Silver Bullet

Next in the transition process is the establishment of an *institution-specific monitoring system* for TTL outcomes of each implemented modification. Such a metric system will generate useful information to guide subsequent TTL innovation brainstorming and commitment. Building a set of *sustainability metrics* makes sustainable business data available for review in a standardized format and allows comparisons of innovations from a variety of sources both inside and outside the organization.

At this point, a common pitfall is to quickly adapt a set of metrics that value a weak set of criteria and ignore the most salient ingredients of the reform process. Another sign of trouble is when an organization immediately boasts its self-acclaimed early success in sustainable business practices. Most concerning is an organization that intentionally disguises superficial changes as sustainable and proceeds to market themselves as a leader in the movement. The transition to a sustainable organization is a lengthy process and requires an honest, institution-wide commitment for constant creative advancement, analysis of outcomes, and continual process enhancement. Today, the most potent organizations in this movement often portray their noteworthy efforts and accomplishments as simply "the way we do business."

Just as the natural world is replete with a wide variety of niches and organisms that fill them, the TTL value process differs from organization to organization. But at the same time, commonalities do emerge throughout all organization types and sizes. For example, a strong institutional initiative normally solves multiple problems — financial, social, and environmental — with some of the resounding benefits completely unplanned and unexpected. On a practical note, what works in one set of circumstances for one organization may not work in another setting for another business; TTL bull's eye solutions are surprisingly specific to a particular set of circumstances. Successful sustainable business innovation seems to evolve and refine not unlike slightly different species niches in slightly different ecosystems. No single boiler plate set of directions exists for all organizations to use to morph into sustainable practices. Rather than the existence of a few reproducible "silver bullets" of sustainable business innovation, the rule appears to be countless silver flecks with similar themes among numerous engaged organizations and companies.

3.7 The Better Part of Valor

A common repercussion associated with many past environmental, social, or business policies has been the unexpected creation of new problems or the exacerbation of existing ones that the policy was intended to remedy, e.g., the proposed augmentation of our petroleum-based vehicle fleet to phase in the use of biofuels (a fuel generally produced from agricultural biomass). Some early purported benefits include a reduction of dependency on crude oil, less pollution from biofuel vehicles, and the additional market demand for farm crops used to produce biofuel.

However, closer examination reveals a number of significant drawbacks that accompany this new technology. The mechanized planting, cultivation, and harvest of biomass materials are accomplished by a farming system that continually degrades soil quality and delivers significant amounts of pesticides into drinking water supplies. The changeover to a biofuel harvest on an agricultural field also decreases proportionately the amount of crop in that farm unit used

1. degrades soil quality + pesticides in water
2. raising food crop prices
3. CO_2 released
4. investment $ $ for little reward.
   Not biomimetic
   5. reliance on fossil fuels

The Bull's Eye   55

as food product, thereby theoretically raising the price of food. When the biofuel is burned in our vehicles, carbon dioxide, a greenhouse gas, is released into the atmosphere. Finally, investment costs for a nationwide system of biofuel production and distribution facilities would be sizeable, and although a biofuel production system would reduce some negative inputs, the overall fallout renders the proposal considerably less than an optimum strategy for our future. In terms of biomimicry, the natural world simply does not combust biomass to power its transportation, and our new-found insight suggests humankind would do well to follow this ageless trend.

Consider the term *renewable energy*. By definition, this term is defined as energy continuously available from natural processes, and biofuels technology, for example, is generally classified as renewable energy. The average citizen concerned with environmental issues likely assumes that all energy sources classified as *renewable* provide an intelligent alternative to fossil fuels and nuclear power. But just as we discussed, serious problems accompany biofuel production such as the reliance upon fossil fuels to deliver the biofuel stock. Modern farming practices also cause significant soil erosion and loss of fertility, soil salinization, over-drafting of aquifers, and the migration of pesticides into our drinking water. Supplementing our fuel stock with biofuel would only provide a modest reduction in crude oil demand and would emit large amounts of carbon dioxide into an atmosphere that is drastically overloaded with 36% more of this greenhouse gas than in pre-industrial times.[11] This example illustrates the misinformation that sometimes accompanies *renewable* energy technologies. Keep in mind that an *alternative* energy choice does not automatically translate to the *best* choice. As mentioned earlier, using a *systems approach* for evaluating new technology options will help elucidate the important considerations for decision makers. *define systems approach?*

So if biofuels do not stand up to careful scrutiny, why has the concept been so vigorously promoted? This question leads us to consider who stands to economically benefit the most from such an energy

---

[11] See U.S. Environmental Protection Agency (2008) for more information about specific amounts and percentages of atmospheric greenhouse gasses.

technology changeover. We find that corporate agriculture, some privately owned farms, investors in biofuel processing companies, and the commercial construction sector stand to gain the most from a boom in biofuels production. And in fact, these entities are leading the promotional charge for a mainstream acceptance of biofuels technology. Unfortunately, outside of this narrow group of winners, most of the human population and all other biota would be much better served by solar or ocean-sourced energy technology.

Supporters of the biofuels controversy are not the only people attempting to ride the metaphoric coat-tails of sustainable business. Mounting public popularity of the movement has enticed some organizations to adapt and vigorously publicize their "green" projects, many of which upon inspection provide little environmental or social benefits. The underlying intent by instigators of these initiatives is often to promote a more positive company image to the public, and in legitimate sustainability circles, this ploy is commonly recognized and referred to as "green-washing." This increasingly common marketing tactic dilutes the integrity, effectiveness, and reputation of the ingenuous sustainable business movement and distracts public attention from more important reform considerations. Fortunately, an increasingly educated and discerning public is becoming better able to identify these movement "pretenders" and to conduct their business associations accordingly. Let us now discuss this topic of current public literacy about the sustainable business movement.

Indeed, judicious consideration of the full technological impact of our options is critical for the success of this movement. A simply different approach to an issue does not necessarily deliver a more desirable result, and alternative energy approaches unabashedly billed as "green" often trade one set of environmental and social problems for another. Businesses engaged in inferior technologies often use disingenuous marketing tactics to win approval and support from an unsuspecting public sector. Writers and editors of various publications, who often lack the comprehensive knowledge required to effectively assess proposed technological changes, may unintentionally misinform by reporting seriously flawed propositions in a positive light. Hopefully, as the movement evolves, refines, and advances, mainstream media expertise of sustainable business will improve as well.

A situation that slows the advancement of the movement is the relatively low level of understanding of the core issues by business leaders and the general public. Developing a solid proficiency in foundational sustainability topics at every level of society would improve our collective ability to intelligently discuss and craft improvements, including private and public policy that would be in the best interest of all people for all times. Clearly, an enhanced awareness of natural and human world themes along with a *systems thinking* approach that identifies and considers all the positive and negative effects of proposed reform upon all living things, will help guide a straighter course to an abundant, vibrant, durable, and fulfilling future. A full range of intriguing formal sustainability education topics and approaches are discussed in Chapter 5.

Business leaders committed to TTL innovation may intend in principle to generate relatively equal outputs of financial, environmental, and social returns for each change they instigate, but with organizations still developing this expertise, one or more of these outcomes are often under-produced. As mentioned earlier, the social component is often lean or sometimes non-existent in practices self-labeled "sustainable." Genuine attempts by business to craft authentic TTL innovations do fall short for a number of reasons, including the lack of a specific requisite technology or simply the limited expertise and creativity of those involved in organizing the effort.

Another limiting factor for the movement maturation process is the common top-down hierarchal approach for organizational management, although successful TTL pioneering efforts have been inspired by executive evangelists, driven by bottom- and middle-tier participants, and facilitated by managers at all levels. Today, companies leading the charge are often organized in much more "flat" operational schemes, with collaborating teams given more responsibility and autonomy for important decisions. An example of this organizational approach is the non-conventional 10-year young company *Google* — the universal information management giant started by Larry Page and Sergey Brin in a Stanford University dorm room.

Indeed, this type of cutting-edge organizational approach facilitates much quicker information sharing and allows more decisions to be made at the level that they originated from. This type of decentralized, nimble, and responsive approach uses the talents and strengths of individuals strategically placed in functioning teams and quite easily adapts to collaborative TTL projects. A potent sustainable business organization routinely provides best-practices education for all staff, offers incentives for TTL innovation, and encourages bottom–up involvement in the reform process.

3.8 The Toyota Way

Many companies initially enter the sustainable business movement because executives see it as an opportunity to increase their profitability and client appeal. Often, early transition initiatives are publicized in green marketing campaigns for the purpose of advancing public image and reputation. Additional organizational innovation provides further TTL returns, including financial, which have given the movement much of its early broad-based traction. For example, the Japanese juggernaut Toyota adapted its signature "just-in-time" manufacturing technology to drastically reduce waste, lower inventories of both parts and assembled products, improve logistical production systems, and raise product quality. In this past decade, Toyota implemented cutting-edge gasoline engine/electric motor hybrid technology in a number of vehicle models and in doing so has set a new industry standard for energy efficiency. These technological changes have translated into increased profits and a positive public image as a "green" auto maker.

That said, it is important to recognize that recent Toyota hybrid innovation has only modestly reduced the adverse effects of petroleum-based combustion-engine technology, which has been seriously flawed from its inception. In short, Toyota has become very good at producing the wrong type of vehicle. The opportunity still exists for some visionary automobile manufacturer to take the lead and produce a comprehensively intelligent and popular vehicle — a sun/wind-powered product of service — with a myriad of full-value-producing

TTL initiatives embedded in the material-cycling production process. This type of industry commitment and changeover also requires the simultaneous development of supporting infrastructure to facilitate such a drastic amendment, with governments providing the correct incentives to these entrepreneurial businesses. To make this transition an all-win reality, human commerce will form the kinds of inter-relationships common in natural world industry: manufacturers working with energy production working with material processors working with take-back systems working with urban planners... and the part-nerships go on and on.

From the second half of the 20th century until the present, while steadily increasing its global market share of vehicles, Toyota leadership has intensely concentrated on increasing productivity at all levels of its domestic manufacturing workforce. The typical Japanese corporate mid-manager and line worker both endure a grueling work schedule, particularly challenging production demands, and fewer workplace amenities when compared to the typical U.S. automobile worker. Illustrating a general disregard for the welfare of Japanese employees is the common executive refer-ence to processing the annual attrition of retiring workers as "tak-ing out the trash." High-level Toyota executives are some of the most influential business leaders in Japan, and when they recognize the value of working conditions that support the employee, a piv-otal change in Japanese business philosophy can occur that will move Toyota, and eventually other attentive Japanese companies, an important step closer to comprehensive TTL sustainable business practices.

3.9 Approaching the Bull's Eye

As mentioned previously, a common pattern for organizations that initiate sustainable business reform is to first adopt efficiency improve-ments that somewhat decrease production costs and environmental damages. A company might then switch some of its operational materials to those that are purported as "environmentally friendly." A computer retailer might begin a take-back program for obsolete computers and monitors with an unintended end result of disadvantaged workers either in the U.S. or abroad disassembling the items and exposing their bodies and the surrounding environment to heavy metals and toxic compounds in the process (durable goods are not yet *designed* to cycle). A particularly ambitious company might even craft a simple metric system that quantifies the cost savings, pollution reduction, and positive publicity generated by each innovation.

These initial modifications, although well-intentioned, usually do not produce significant TTL value and essentially duplicate measures by some businesses during the last few decades of the environmental movement. *Lean production* and *total quality management* are examples of early, narrowly focused strategies that were designed to eliminate any portion of a production process that did not produce economic value. Although these processes might sound enticing, missing are positive and restorative industrial contributions to the natural world and to human communities. The definition of quality is deficient in both approaches. To paraphrase visionary architect and designer William McDonough, being less bad is still bad... just less so.

A thorough understanding of the core principles of sustainable business will enable us to effectively engage in a purely positive and cooperative system of human endeavor. This lofty and idealistic goal is pushing a variety of organizations past the initial transition stages and forward into a transformation unparalleled in the history of man. At this point, the ability to understand the challenges and to think and commit "outside the box" are two key factors for determining the extent and quality of our remaining tenure on Earth.

In their 1999 book, *Natural Capitalism*, Paul Hawken, Amory Lovins, and L. Hunter Lovins deftly point out that most organizations do not typically promote and reward *creativity and originality* by their employees. Providing a working environment conducive to TTL innovation is a powerful tool for plucky business leaders that can help a company move much deeper into the transformation process. A comfortable workplace, a performance assessment category in creativity, and regular collaboration opportunities with other employees are just three examples that facilitate valuable innovation. Redesigning worker evaluations to include expectations such as

collaborative redesign contributions and sustainable business educational activities would directly connect individual TTL engagement with professional advancement. With pioneering business leaders now redesigning for three types of value instead of simply pushing profitability and tossing the environment and their employees an occasional bone, successful and durable businesses of the future will embed *a continuous cycle of enhancement and evaluation* into their day-to-day operations. Formally engaging and rewarding TTL process in the workplace is one strategy that will help to drive a positive and lasting rehabilitation of our business culture. *efficiency improvements*
≠ potential SB. Initial modifications ≠ significant TTL value goals to get past initial transitions, to true transformation. . . .

3.10 Intelligent Building Design

Perhaps the most commonly recognizable component of the sustainable business movement is facility design. For the general public today, "building green" perhaps represents the essence of the sustainability movement, and certainly the evolving sustainability paradigm will naturally be reflected in the architecture of personal and commercial structures. The most prominent national program involved in environmentally and socially intelligent building design is *Leadership in Energy and Environmental Design* (LEED) of the U.S. Green Building Council (USGBC), a 501(c)(3) non-profit organization. With over 75 USGBC local chapters scattered throughout nearly every state, the LEED program offers a voluntary third-party benchmark and rating system for the design and construction of both residential and commercial facilities. LEED offers a green-building performance evaluation by using human and environmental health, water use, energy choices, and building materials selection as the main criteria.

Since the LEED program inception in 1996, considerable progress has been made by the USGBC to develop, publicize, and promote green-building practices. By 2006, over 800 commercial structures and nearly 200 residential buildings were LEED-certified at various levels and more than 12,000 building projects had applied for certification. The USGBC is further expanding the scope of LEED certification to include guidelines for the development of residential neighborhoods and even college campuses. Although much progress has been made in this field, considerably more opportunities remain to further develop more region-specific criteria and even better design standards.

Some visionary architects and engineers are designing "beyond LEED" with the elimination of all polyvinyl chloride (PVC) building materials, interior noise reduction features, and a variety of location-appropriate design characteristics not currently recognized by the LEED program. Hopefully, the USGBC will continue to build upon its approach to facility and community design and use its current high profile to advance the sustainability movement with integrity and imagination. If the LEED program stalls at providing full TTL rating criteria, we can expect other building design organizations to step up and establish richer TTL design standards for third-party rating systems. William McDonough asserts that design is the first signal of our intentions; so appropriately, the design of our buildings will not only reflect our profound respect for all occupants but will also celebrate our connections with all communities for all times.

Up to this point, our discussion has covered energy choices, material usage, and building design. The touchstone for longstanding value includes three basic elements — profitability, the planet, and people. For all but the most committed organizations, TTL reform has been minimal to this point. In the next chapter, we will examine many of the actual frontrunners in the sustainable business movement and look at how investing in employees, community, and the natural world has increased profits and improved the long-term market position of individual companies.

The environmental legislation of the latter part of the 20th century sought to reduce the pernicious industrial side effects cast upon humanity and the natural world. As previously mentioned, environmentalists instigated these reforms, but now, in hindsight, we are beginning to realize that marginally reducing our negative industrial outcomes does not go far enough. At the same time, leaders in business constantly strive to reduce the risk associated with significant changes in process and practice. The systemic reform incumbent upon the sustainable business movement does overwhelm some stakeholders, so the aversion to risk quite often translates into reduced levels of commitment. But as new TTL ideas surface and prove themselves, advancements will continue in many organizations, at least in the short term. Furthermore, mainstream financial investment toward sustainable practices has only begun, and the emergence of a broadly shared new industrial paradigm is indeed on the horizon. *We are learning that the advancement of business, the natural world, and our citizens need not be at the expense of one another.* Continued progress will certainly require constant scrutiny, adjustments, and thoughtfully pursued innovation, but growing reasons for optimism are evident. The magnitude of the transformation will certainly require many decades of changeover; indeed, the first industrial revolution took nearly three centuries to mature, so designing our way out of our deep and serious problems will require considerable time, effort, creativity, and resources, with the natural world as our guide.

Beyond LEED: ·eliminate PVC, ·reduce interior noise, locality addressed. Risk involved w/ TTL scares stakeholders.

3.11 Urgent Challenges, Appropriate Remedies

Another key consideration for the evolution of this movement is the relative urgency associated with each of the specific crises that we now face. Both the extent of current damage and the risk of future harm vary in terms of each predicament as sometimes does the time remaining to address the problem. Authoring a prioritized list of our industrial dilemmas to guide the sequence of remediation is strategically important. Not only are fitting corrective measures needed, but equally critical are the order and combination in which we execute these changes. We can compare such prioritizing to triage by an emergency room physician: first treat a patient's life-threatening injuries before tending to any superficial cuts and abrasions.

In this context, let us consider the well-publicized international, inter-species, and inter-age topic of global climate change. In the early 1980s, a small group of scientists raised the profile of a century-old hypothesis that humans had been influencing natural global climate patterns by burning massive amounts of fossil fuels for many decades and thereby emitting increasing quantities of greenhouse gasses in the process. Since then, numerous teams of research climatologists around the world have constructed sophisticated computer programs that model Earth's climatic responses to changes in the various atmospheric greenhouse gas levels over the last 150 years. Greenhouse gasses make up much less than 1% of the atmosphere but are responsible for absorbing a large part of the incoming long-wave solar radiation (heat). This "greenhouse effect" warms Earth's average surface temperature by 60° Fahrenheit (45° Celsius), enabling liquid water to exist over much of the Earth most of the time. These gasses also make the atmosphere conducive to life by moderating the high and low temperature swings of day and night and of the changing seasons away from the equatorial latitudes.

Predicted effects of climate change from these sophisticated computer models include rising ocean levels, an increase in the temperature and a subsequent decrease in the carbon-holding capacity of the oceans, an increase in the frequency and intensity of hurricanes/ typhoons, changing global precipitation patterns, and eventual new locations of productive farmland. Perhaps the most surprising and alarming possibility suggested by the models is a rapid shift to an extended ice age considerably sooner than would otherwise take place, resulting in hundreds of feet of ice and snow eventually covering much of the U.S. throughout an entire year. The only scientific controversy still remaining among nearly all reputable climate-change scientists is not whether significant climate change will occur but how soon and to what extent these changes will happen.

Perhaps the critical question concerning climate change is whether the possibility still exists to *prevent* such a cascade of catastrophic events. Carbon dioxide, an atmospheric greenhouse gas, has already increased more than one-third from its pre-1850 concentration, and other more potent greenhouse gas concentrations have also risen sharply during that same period. The United Nations' Kyoto Accord Treaty, finally ratified in November 2004, requires developed nations (except the U.S. and Australia which did not ratify the treaty) to reduce the 1990 emissions of six greenhouse gasses by 5.2% by 2012. Developing nations, including China and India, are responsible only for annually reporting their greenhouse gas emissions and not reducing the amounts. This international agreement might have been appropriate 100 years ago, but relying upon these sorts of reductions today will prove too little too late to avoid the aforementioned calamitous events. Some of the leading scientists in climatology now tell us much more change is needed very soon in order to significantly reduce the risk of catastrophic global climate change.

Ironically, many improvements in energy efficiency and transitions to clean energy options will provide an attractive rate of payback today without even considering the positive contributions to climate change. Reductions in air, water, and soil pollution from fossil fuel use will eliminate countless deaths, health ailments, medical costs, loss of work time, and loss of crop productivity, just to name a few. If we include the effects on the prospect of climate change, the rewards are overwhelming even if we consider only the best interests of our own species. Incidentally, ten to fifteen million other existing species will inherit the consequences of our action no matter what direction we choose.

Global climate change is an example of an imminent and reasonable threat that commands a high priority for many members of the international community. Most readers of this book are familiar with the concept of risk avoidance; we often choose to eat healthy foods and exercise regularly at least in part to avoid the health problems that accompany obesity. Most of us would choose seat belts regardless of the law requiring their use because we know the data say we are at less risk to serious injury when we do so. We do not angrily storm out of our vehicles after using our seat belts if we do not get into an accident when we are prepared for one; rather, we are more comfortable putting ourselves in a situation with a lower risk. Why would we treat the threat associated with global climate change differently?

Any rational plan to significantly reduce the risk associated with global climate change will be expedient and substantial. To capitulate on an issue of this magnitude for the sake of convenience or expense would be gambling with the very conditions conducive to life on Earth as we know it. Accepting the likely consequences of inaction and the quickly closing window of opportunity is a reality that challenges our current generation. Settling for measures that do not provide a reasonable expectation of remedy but do require considerable time, international attention, and resources is not in the best interest of humanity. Hopefully, international commitment will deepen and broaden very soon in this regard. In another analogy, we would certainly not be satisfied with protection in a head-on crash from a seat belt made out of a few strands of kite string; similarly, cursory measures are not acceptable for an impending global head-on collision with the next ice age.

3.12   Early Organizational Change

The initial attempts by an organization to adopt TTL practices generally garner only modest results such as a minor reduction in pollution, slightly lowered operating costs, and little or no social benefits. Subsequent early changes are also typically conservative and relatively low risk. Payback times for the accompanying financial investments are given close scrutiny by decision makers, and environmental and social dividends are generally secondary concerns. These beginning incremental initiatives fall into the category of *transition strategies* and generally move the organization only slightly in the evolution of a sustainable business. Transitional strategies are planned methods for changing the characteristics and operations of an organization that profitably reduce harm or provide value to the natural world, the workforce, and human community. As these newly engaged organizations accomplish small but laudable projects, the tangible payback results may help "prime the pump" for even more meaningful innovation. Sometimes a business serious about transitioning chooses to channel the revenue generated into a separate account that is used to fund further TTL changes. Under the right combination of top-level commitment and acquired sustainable practices moxie, financial resources for TTL innovation can increase fairly rapidly in this scenario. In other organizations, the financial capital is routed into the general financial fund and successive innovation is typically implemented at a somewhat slower rate.

At this stage, after a few early minor-level changes have proven their worth, decision makers often become more comfortable and move a bit more aggressively toward TTL goals. If the campaign is led

[handwritten note: prime the pump = save money from initial modifications to help carrying on bigger transformations]

by a particularly zealous and knowledgeable movement champion, further examination of the operation reveals new innovation opportunities. At this point, most organizational change is fairly simple, low risk, and demonstrates tangible but limited TTL value production. These relatively straightforward opportunities are often labeled "low hanging fruit" and raise the comfort and confidence levels of both change proponents and less confident team members alike. By this time, leaders may feel satisfied with their initial success, even to the point of complacency. After all, in most cases, competitors have not enjoyed nearly as much sustainable business progress. While at the same time, more focused leaders find that early success inspires further commitment for moving the organization even further into a sustainable business metamorphosis. Taking a deeper plunge requires an intrepid scrutiny of business-as-usual, with both the perceived risks and potential rewards considerably higher. Let us now investigate some tools, processes, and approaches that will assist the engaged organization in reaching even greater heights and accomplishments.

3.13 The Score Card

As company leaders consider various proposed changes to established processes and structure, they generally prefer viewing the "hard numbers" that represent the performance rating of past sustainable business initiatives by their company. Change agents also find access to such quantitative data about other transitioning organizations useful and encouraging. Not surprisingly, some committed companies have already taken the initiative to develop an internal system of sustainable business metrics. This sustainability scorecard process is supported by selected staff members with the explicit responsibility of bringing teams of employees together to identify innovation opportunities, designing an ongoing series of TTL projects; and embedding all approved schemes into the fabric of the operation. TTL performance data are then compiled and shared with all staff members, including the highest level of company officers. The design and complexity of the operational metric system vary according to organization type, size, and sustainable business expertise, but the following example illustrates a simple generic metrics system that can act as a starting point for internal use and for comparison among a variety of organizations.

Two-Part Sustainable Business Metric System		
General Class Rating:		
Red	0% to 19% energy from sustainable sources and less than 5% of output POS or POC produced or used in operations	
Orange	20% to 49% energy from sustainable sources and if manufacturing, 5% or more POS or POC output products or if service, 5% or more durable goods used in operations POS or POC	
Yellow	50% to 99% energy from sustainable sources and if manufacturing, only POS or POC-output products or if service, only POS or POC used in operations	
White	100% energy from sustainable sources and if manufacturing, only POS or POC output products or if service, only POS or POC used in operations and locally owned and controlled	
Running Point Score:	**Minor Innovation****	**Major Innovation***
	2 points for financial, social, and environmental value produced	10 points for financial, social, and environmental value produced

(*Continued*)

(Continued)

*Major Innovation =	1% increase of base line profits; significant and verifiable benefits to local biota; significant benefits to employees and local community
**Minor Innovation =	Verifiable value in three categories but less than needed for major innovation

SB Education:

15 points for a comprehensive sustainable business education program for top-level employees
30 points for a comprehensive sustainable business education program for all employees

An Example:

Acme Widget Company produces 25% of their stationary and transportation energy demand from the sun and wind. Half of the widgets it produces are products of consumption. Company leaders have established a comprehensive sustainable business education program for top-level employees. Since implementing the metric system two years ago, the organization has implemented two programs that satisfy the requirements for major innovation and six programs that satisfy the requirements for minor innovation.

Currently, Acme Widget Company has a general class metric rating of orange with a running point score of 47.

This simple metric system example is included to serve as a straightforward and instructive model for tabulating a meaningful running indication of sustainable business innovation performance. This example does require subjective interpretation for terms such as "significant and verifiable benefits" and a "comprehensive sustainable business education program," which can be more strictly defined as the need arises. This basic model omits other possible criteria items such as the TTL design characteristics of company buildings or the

TTL performance of associated sub-contracting and supply-chain companies. Also, items not specifically included can sometimes enter the calculation as separate major or minor TTL innovations.

A number of metric systems for sustainable practices are now in use including the extensive sustainability standards adopted in 2008 by The Business and Institutional Furniture Manufacturing Association (BIFMA). Some weaknesses of early metric systems include the concentration on lowering negative inputs to the natural world accompanied by the lack of emphasis on positive contributions to nature as well as the low priority assigned to social value production. Nevertheless, existing sustainability metric systems or their components may have utility for those organizations that are looking for ideas to include in the crafting of their own performance score cards.

3.14 A Helping Hand

Companies can surpass their internal capacity for meaningful TTL change relatively quickly. Most companies discover that, even with individual movement champions, they have limited movement theory expertise practical transition experience and soon find efforts at a standstill. When this happens, where can organization leaders turn for assistance in moving deeper and broader into rewarding change for sustainable business? Fortunately, a handful of competent non-profit and for-profit consulting organizations now offer custom consulting and training in sustainable business. Indeed, organizations that are sincere can jumpstart their transition efforts by hiring reputable sustainable business consultants at a wide range of fees and service levels.

The most difficult part of this process is often finding a suitable consultant that matches the organization's intentions and budget. Some regions of the U.S. offer a richer portfolio of choices for advisory work than others, but the number of qualified (and, unfortunately, less qualified) professionals will no doubt continue to grow throughout most major metropolitan areas. Locating a competent sustainable business consulting service is often a formidable task for the interested organization. Many times, the most pressing need inside a company is to convey a clear understanding of the fundamentals of sustainable business to key professionals, so both a solid grasp of movement principles and the ability to effectively educate are critical skills for the consultant. The consultant selection process presents quite a challenge for the interested company to find someone who has this skill set plus the ability to apply movement theory to the specific situation and operation of the company. As with all types of consultant assistance, interested organizations would do well to compare the formal education, relevant experience, and the deliverable product quality of those professionals they are considering.

3.15 Staff Roles in the Transition

With the relevance and utility of sustainable business extending from multinational corporations to sole-proprietor businesses and from non-profits to all levels of government, each separate series of organizational change will be correspondingly diverse. However, some commonalities within business sectors and among organizations themselves are also appearing during this tumultuous transition process. The following summary of selected employee positions found inside many organizations outlines new duties and collaborative relationships among previously segregated staff members. Although the position responsibility varies inside organizations and the sequence of change will differ from business to business, these examples demonstrate the oncoming challenges and strategic insight for beginning the redeployment of personnel into intelligent roles in transitioning companies. The following provides a generic glimpse into the changing professional responsibilities that accompany this redesign of business endeavors:

Accountants: These professionals are trained in a system of recording and summarizing business and financial transactions and analyzing, verifying, and reporting the results. This expertise is important because it supplies useful information about the ongoing viability of an organization. One common monitoring responsibility is reporting the state of industrial capital, financial capital, and human capital. Until recently, conventional accounting practices have ignored reporting another indispensable type — *natural capital* — which includes the living members and non-living parts of natural communities and provides services that deliver the essential conditions needed for life (such as oxygen, climate, and fertile soil), and therefore business, on Earth. Accountants face a particular challenge in reporting the circumstances concerning Earth's natural capital because, unlike the other forms of capital, natural capital often has no existing possibility for replacement. So assigning a monetary value for natural capital that assumes replacement options at a certain price is misleading. The adaptation of meaningful units that allow useful comparisons with other types of capital is one challenge for all sustainable business accounting departments.

Another challenging situation facing the accountant is developing a workable *full-cost accounting system* that assigns all costs to the purchase price of a delivered good or service. For example, the price we pay today at the pump for a gallon of gasoline is far below the actual cost of the fuel. Many other people not directly involved in the economic transaction collectively pay a large part of the cost because of the distant effects of pollution. Similar accounting problems exist for many other financial transactions, and a properly functioning full-cost accounting system would provide much richer information and impetus for intelligent economic decisions by both consumers and producers.

Lastly, accountants will ultimately be responsible for summarizing the financial, social, and natural world value generated by the activities of the organization. While the financial reporting duties will change little, the two new TTL components will provide opportunities for the development of creative and effective accounting procedures that will serve the decision makers and change agents. Eventually, a uniform accounting system for commercial organizations will evolve that will allow meaningful TTL value comparisons across all business sectors.

Marketing and Sales Staff: Once a company begins modifying its DNA by adapting TTL change, the opportunity to benefit from this transformation exists for both marketing specialists and sales staff.

The sustainable business movement is now garnering mainstream recognition around the world and has found its way into an increasing number of public conversations. Movement-engaged companies are enjoying a variety of tangible benefits over conventional business, and one potential reward is an improved public image. Organizations that profitably restore the natural world while building durable and beautiful human communities are attractive to an increasing number of astute Americans, Europeans, Asians, and Africans. Sales staff can include an honest summary of efforts made by their company in conversations with potential clients. Marketing staff have the opportunity to craft a strategic promotional plan that successfully conveys sustainable business initiatives to potential clients. Getting the word out to prospective customers is effective and allows the engaged public to patronize organizations that share their basic values and vision.

Human Resource Specialists: HR specialists will find long-term value from hiring people familiar with and interested in the sustainable business movement and from arranging ongoing staff education in this regard. More and more, HR specialists are asked to craft new programs that develop, motivate, and reward employees and that facilitate a loyal and productive workforce. HR professionals will find themselves serving on TTL innovation teams and will be asked to contribute effective means of building social capital for the organization. Their overarching responsibility and involvement with the entire workforce places the HR specialists in a unique position to improve the sustainable business expertise of the average worker so that the most informed, creative, and valuable staff possible is constantly assembled for company leaders.

Operations Managers: The required retooling of core business practices impacts the operations manager perhaps more than any other position. For these production leaders, a comprehensive and thorough understanding of sustainable business is essential. Operations managers assist in the training of employees in sustainable business principles, provide practical input to TTL innovation teams, and set approved innovation plans into motion while maintaining product quality standards, monitoring performance metric systems, and maintaining regular communication with top executives. Effective managers thoroughly understand the mission of the company, the tenets of authentic sustainable business, and the value of creative "out-of-the-box" approaches for applying movement theory to operations practice. Managing production of three kinds of value rather than the lone profit motive indeed proves quite challenging but professionally rewarding for the operations manager. In short, top executives make sure the company vision of sustainable business is clear; the operations manager makes sure sustainable business innovation is implemented correctly.

Organization Leaders: Maintaining a clear vision is indeed within the purview of company leaders, as is maintaining transition momentum. Organizations that fully leverage the opportunities offered by the movement are most likely driven by clear and consistent directives from top officers. When the leadership sets a high expectation bar for transitional outcomes and provides the necessary resources for success, companies are likely to demonstrate remarkable progress toward these ends. Leaders constantly balance risk avoidance and maverick initiatives that offer high TTL opportunity for the organization. Directing the emergence of company process and culture that consistently delivers creativity, collaboration, profitability, natural world partnership, and community support is indeed a formidable task that requires informed, inspired, confident, and determined leaders.

New Position — Ecologists: Now committed to a natural world partnership, organizations quickly realize that management lacks a clear understanding of how nature works. Ecologists, who are well-versed in the local natural community, are hired to assist in the proper design of business processes that generate environmental value. Using a natural-world perspective, ecologists will join the design team and provide suggestions on how to best engage, restore, and support local ecosystems. Until public education systems deliver business graduates who understand the nature of nature, transitioning companies will have a need for ecology specialists to actively participate in TTL process design.

New Position — Sociologists: Organizations now committed to a human community partnership discover a need for skilled consultants who will guide the direction of social-value creation in TTL efforts. Acting as ambassadors for the human community, sociologists recommend how the business can best interface with and contribute to the fabric of local society. The social scientist assists the TTL innovation team by suggesting and evaluating the various alternatives for community involvement and enrichment. Properly conceived, initiatives are win-win situations for both the community and the organization. Flexibility, business expertise, imagination, and a collaborative spirit are qualities that serve business-focused sociologists inside the transitioning business environment.

New Position — Sustainable Business Directors: Top-level organization leaders sometimes find that evangelizing sustainable business practices is a full-time job that requires constant attention and tutelage. The addition of a formally trained, full-time campaigner who reports directly to the CEO (or equivalent) and who oversees all the sustainable business efforts of the organization can make the difference between moderate and exemplary transition outcomes. The successful sustainable business director is the consummate *comprehensivist* with expertise in conventional business, science, environmental studies, and authentic sustainable business. This big-picture change agent is familiar with the nebulous connections among business, nature, and the built environment. Ideally, this key position is filled with a graduate of one of the few legitimate sustainable business undergraduate or graduate programs in existence. Such an individual will not have direct experience working inside the specific organization, but as the first order of business, he or she will become familiar with the operation. In addition to a deep familiarity with the foundations of sustainable business, successful directors possess exceptional organization leadership and communication skills, imagination, as well as charisma, the ability to work both independently and collaboratively. A capable and potent director of sustainable business will drive the genetic change inside the organization, dispel apathy and complacency, and maintain positive change momentum for TTL value.

Thus far we have examined the conceptual considerations supporting the sustainable business movement and applied these concepts to a limited number of real-world cases. In our next chapter, we will examine many current examples of organizations that have intrepidly begun the sustainable business transition, organizations spanning the range of mom-and-pop-owned local businesses to medium-sized and large corporations. We will look at how cutting-edge entrepreneurs on five continents have put the ideas of sustainable business to work as value-producing, competitive advantage mechanisms for their company, their community, and the natural world.

Guide Point 3: The incremental transition of an organization to sustainable practices that is rooted in TTL innovation and guided by nature-based precepts will simultaneously build durable commerce and thriving communities for all species for all times.

Chapter 4

Businesses Taking Care of Business

Thus far, we have considered the tumultuous environmental and social problems brought on by the unplanned expansion of the first Industrial Revolution. We are aware that the opportunity to experience a high quality of life is diminishing with each passing generation. Fortunately, we have also learned that a groundswell reform of business and our communities is now coalescing and beginning to tackle these fundamental problems. A case was made that supports the wisdom of emulating natural world industrial strategies in our new design plan for human industry and communities around the globe. Benevolent, nourishing, and community-supporting industry is our goal and we can use the various tools and methods suggested in earlier chapters to facilitate meaningful systemic organizational change.

Private enterprise is actively leading the reform. Numerous engaged organizations and communities around the world have already converted their operations to yield considerable TTL value production, with some already flourishing in their newly established intentions. Sustainable business has extended into the mainstream conversations and culture of American and European societies. No longer are these bold reform ideas merely conceptual; they are now embedded and performing splendidly in a wide variety of commercial and community settings. You may be wondering what, if any, the role of government is in this pivotal movement. We will tackle that conundrum in a later chapter; for now, know that the role of government is to enact intelligent policy incentives and disincentives to help drive and direct change.

This chapter features numerous real-world examples of diverse businesses that have incorporated remarkably effective processes yielding consistent financial, natural world, and social rewards.

Although the following collection of profiled organizations is only a small sample of the broad ingenuity and commitment found in this movement, these illustrations will provide interesting and informative examples of the emerging face of sustainable business. Additionally, these real-world cases are snapshots in time compiled in late 2008; continued organizational evolution in each instance is assumed. Hopefully, these assorted descriptions of TTL innovation put into practice will inform and inspire new participants who will put forth another wave of fearless transformations that will permeate and fill every business sector.

4.1 United States For-Profit Companies

New Belgium Brewery, Fort Collins, CO — Beer Brewery

This mid-sized beer brewery was founded in 1991 by electrical engineer Jeff Lebesch and his wife, social worker Kim Jordan. A full-time sustainability officer position anchors the brewery's commitment to transitioning to sustainable business practices. The company generates 10%–15% of its electricity by burning the methane produced by bacteria at the on-site water purification plant, and the remaining 85%–90% of electrical demand is mitigated by the purchase of a corresponding amount of wind energy credits. These credits pay the difference between the cost of conventionally generated electricity and the higher cost of wind-generated electricity at a distant Wyoming facility. Brewery employees voted unanimously to use profit-sharing funds to finance the wind energy credits. During the winter months, induction fans draw in cold outside air to help cool the beer. In the warm months, evaporative coolers condition the air in the 55,000-square-feet packaging hall, so the need for energy-intensive refrigeration compressors is avoided. The company researched and implemented the most efficient brewing procedures; consequently, it saves over $3,000 per month on off-site energy purchases and reduces carbon emissions by 8 million pounds per year.

Innovation teams have also reduced company water use (in short supply in this part of Colorado) by 50% through various recapture programs. Today, New Belgium uses only four gallons of water to brew a gallon of beer while the industry average is eight to 10 gallons.[12] Spent grain from the brewing process is diverted from the company waste stream and sent to local farms where it is used as animal feed. Natural daylight from numerous windows, light tubes, and light shelves illuminates the indoor brewery facilities, and energy-saving motion sensor switches for electrical lighting are installed in most locations. Natural indirect daylight is diffuse, soft, and easy on the eye, while an illuminating surprising amount surface detail for the employees. The interior walls of the packaging facility are made with locally procured beetle-killed pine lumber. New Belgium contributes 1% of total sales receipts to environmental non-profit organizations. Furthermore, this company gives each employee a new custom-built bike after one year of employment. In order to serve as an accessible business role model, the company offers on-site tours daily and off-site presentations as requested by local schools and organizations.

New Seasons Market, Portland, OR — Grocery Stores

This locally owned and operated company has nine store locations in the Portland area, nearly 1,800 employees, and an annual revenue of over $37 million. Founded in 1999 by Brian Rohter and Stan Amy, New Seasons Market (NSM) aspires to be the friendliest store in the Portland metro area and specializes in organic and health foods along with a variety of conventional grocery products. All NSM store bakeries are certified organic, and about one-third of the items offered in NSM stores are grown or manufactured in the Pacific Northwest. Plastic grocery bags have never been offered at any of the stores, and in 2008, more than a quarter of its customers received five cents for each grocery bag they brought in for transporting their groceries. Once a week from June through October, each store hosts five to seven local growers who bring in unique produce, homemade cheeses, and microbrew beers.

---

[12] See New Belgium Brewing Company (2008).

Each of the nine stores has an employee "green team" that works on continuous improvements that have included cycling and repro- cessing systems, energy efficiency, waste reduction, and community and staff education. Ten percent of after-tax profits are donated to various community organizations. Each store provides three volun- teers per day to serve shut-in senior citizens for the Meals-On-Wheels program, with three stores using only bicycles in the process. Two full-time nutritionists are hired by the company to teach wellness classes free of charge to all community members. New Season Market also supports their employees by providing loans of $200 to $2,500 for unexpected life situations regardless of the employee's credit history.

Google, Mountain View, CA — Internet Information Access

Google was founded in 1998 by Larry Page and Sergey Brin near the southernmost extension of San Francisco Bay in California. This multi-billion dollar publicly-traded corporation provides all types of easily accessible world information via Internet search engines. With nearly 20,000 employees worldwide, Google earns revenue from advertising that is packaged inside various information search engines and services. Google adapts and grows using a loosely formed and flat corporate hierarchy with nearly all employees responsible for many different types of projects. For example, Google engineers spend one day per week working on special projects that particularly interest them, and this freedom of choice has resulted in some of the newer services offered, such as Gmail and Google News. Google work facil- ities are certainly non-conventional: offices are arranged in clusters of three to four workers and are furnished with couches; bicycles are commonly parked in hallways; workout facilities with exercise machines and shower rooms are standard; ping-pong and rollerblade hockey games are common; free healthy meals and snacks are avail- able throughout the day in community cafeterias; on-site day care, massage, dentistry, and health care services are provided; and mater- nity and paternity leave is also available to employees.

Most facilities have abundant natural lighting, energy-management software, and evaporative cooling schemes. At the Google world headquarters in Mountain View, CA, leaders have installed a photovoltaic system of over 9,000 solar panels on the top of eight buildings and two carports that generates 30% of peak power demand; this system will pay for itself in 78 months and will continue to provide electricity for decades thereafter. All workers that walk, bike, or commute via mass transit to and from the headquarters complex can participate in a complimentary car-sharing program. Google's commitment to continuous innovation and to maintaining a small-business atmosphere that values individuals and their abilities, product performance, and intelligent energy choices bodes well for the long-term future of this highly profitable information heavyweight.

Patagonia, Ventura, CA — Outdoor Performance Clothing

In 1970, Chouinard Equipment, the predecessor organization of Patagonia, began championing sustainable business values when it decided to stop producing hard metal pitons for rock-climbing that were disfiguring rock walls and instead to manufacture aluminum climbing chocks that left the rock walls in near pristine condition. Patagonia founder Yvon Chouinard then made the decision to stop producing climbing hardware and to begin the design and production of high-performance outdoor clothing for rock and alpine climbing, backpacking, fly fishing, Nordic skiing, downhill skiing, and hiking. Recent year revenues for Patagonia are in the $250–$300 million range. A few highlights from Patagonia's long legacy of cutting-edge business innovation include the following: the opening of one of the first on-site employee day care centers in the U.S. in 1984, eliminating private offices in the same year to improve employee collaboration and communication, giving 1% of total sales revenue since 1985 to community-centered environmental groups to the tune of over $26 million, educating the public on a different sustainability theme each year by including articles in Patagonia merchandise catalogs and on the company Website, and allowing company employees a paid leave of two months to work for an environmental or sustainability organization of their choice. In 2006, the company began treating its wool products in a patented slow-wash process that eliminates the use of chlorine (toxin) and replaced the use of silver (heavy metal pollutant) for anti-microbial odor control with crushed crab and shrimp shells, with no loss of product performance quality.

Yvon Chouinard also understands the value of the people that work for him. He is an avid surfer and has started a custom of extending lunch break time when "surf's up" so employees may hit the waves at the company headquarters located on the Pacific Coast in Ventura, CA. Patagonia also has a history of sponsoring numerous employee skiing and climbing trips throughout California and many other parts of the world. Some employees with unique situations enjoy flexible working schedules and job-sharing arrangements. This type of employee support has yielded a fiercely loyal workforce and a reputation for Patagonia as a wonderful place to work. Today, when a position becomes available at one of Patagonia's facilities, literally hundreds of job applications are submitted. But undoubtedly, employee performance expectations are exacting at Patagonia, and only the most productive, imaginative, and committed individuals are invited to carry on the extraordinary tradition.

In 2006, Patagonia built a new shipping and distribution center in Reno, Nevada with energy efficiency features that reduced conventional energy consumption by one-third. At the Ventura, CA headquarters, purchases Chouinard wind energy credits for half of its electrical demand, and he has installed 360 photovoltaic solar panels on-site to produce another 12% of its electrical needs. In addition to the product-of-service take-back system for all worn-out Capilene® garments mentioned in a previous chapter, in 1996, Patagonia became one of the first major cotton garment producers to use only organically grown cotton for garments and they found that sales of these items rose 25%. With the financial success of Patagonia throughout the years, the company remains 100% privately owned by Chouinard. He has been approached many times by prospective buyers but has shunned all these lucrative offers. By preserving sole ownership, he has maintained control of Patagonia's legacy of solid profitability and contributing to a healthy natural world and human community.

Timberland, Inc., Stratham, NH — Footwear and Outdoor Clothing

Started in 1973, this New England-based company primarily manufactures boots and outdoor clothing, and it surpassed $1 billion in sales in 2007. Timberland has reduced energy consumption at its largest facilities by 40% and has also substantially reduced the use of toxic solvents and adhesives in its products. The company's distribution center in Ontario, CA has a photovoltaic system that generates 60% of the on-site electricity demand. In 2004, Timberland began offering a $3,000 stipend for employees who choose to purchase a hybrid vehicle. The most distinguishing sustainable business project of the company came in 2007 when Timberland introduced its Green Index™ rating system for many products, which includes a sliding scale of 1–10 for climate impact, hazardous chemicals used, and natural resource consumption (more products were included in this system in 2008). By including the scores with each of Timberland's products, this company's leaders set new standards for environmental transparency to retail customers by providing an at-a-glance product comparison of natural world perturbations.

GoLite LLC, Boulder, CO — Outdoor Clothing and Equipment

Company founders Kim and Demetri Coupounas set out in 1998 to produce the best lightweight outdoor clothing and backpacking equipment possible. A task force with a dedicated budget now leads sustainable business initiatives at GoLite. One of their noteworthy accomplishments has been to help establish a regional, multi-company polyester reprocessing center that serves Boulder, CO and other Front Range, Colorado communities. Internally, GoLite has developed the EcoWisp™ and ConsciousBody™ lines of clothing, which are produced from 100% reprocessed polyester. Furthermore, DriMove™ performance fabric, made with activated carbon from waste coconut shells, is used for a number of other company clothing items.

Employees for GoLite who ride bicycles to work can store them inside company buildings and use the showers and locker rooms provided for commuters. Full-time employees are offered one extra week of paid time off per year to volunteer for non-profit environmental organizations to field test company products. GoLite also contributes 1% of all revenues to non-profit companies dedicated to natural-area preservation.

Aveda, Blaine MN — Hair Care, Skin Care, and Makeup Products

Privately founded in 1978 and now owned by Estée Lauder Companies, Aveda expounds the three components of TTL through its mission statement, and the company has practices and policies that do indeed reflect that commitment. Sold in 26 countries, Aveda hair, skin, and make-up products are manufactured using 100% wind power from 19 wind farms in Minnesota. The corporate headquarters and distribution center are also powered by these wind power sources. Additionally, Aveda evaluates over 600 of its product ingredients for human and environmental safety and requires life-cycle analysis when designing merchandise packaging options. (Life-cycle analysis provides information, among other things that allows Aveda to select the least harmful packaging materials.) Prohibited materials for all products and packaging include polyvinyl chloride (PVC), heavy metals, and virgin forest products.

Aveda has entered into some interesting partnerships to ensure product ingredients come from sustainable sources. For example, oil from the fruit of the rare Moroccan argan tree that is used in some skin care products is acquired from a cooperative of Berber women in Morocco. Only fruits fallen on the ground are gathered and processed by the women, with the spent fruit parts given to livestock and the hard shell cases burned as heating fuel. The Berber cooperative is involved in an argan reforestation project for the region and is currently supported by an Aveda two–year grant for new equipment and literacy training. Another indigenous-culture partnership involves the Mardu people of Australia and the responsible harvest of sandalwood, a medium-sized tree with wood that has a pleasurable scent and medicinal qualities. Aveda extracts the active ingredients of the sandalwood using a steam process rather than petrochemical solvents.

Each year in April, Aveda employees worldwide raise money for, and contribute to, various environmental grassroots organizations, such as Greenhouse Network, Clean Air-Cool Planet, and Gulf Coast Restoration Network. Since 1999, company efforts have donated more than $11 million for these and dozens more non-profit organizations.

Frito-Lay, Plano, TX — Snack Food Production

This $11 billion per year division of Pepsi-Co Inc. manufactures the familiar Lays, Ruffles, Doritos, Fritos, SunChips, and Cheetos brands of snack chips. Frito-Lay has concentrated efforts on energy and water-system improvements throughout its facilities. A rooftop solar water heater produces two-thirds of the hot water used by the corporate headquarters in Plano, Texas. The Frito-Lay service center in Phoenix, AZ has over 1,000 photovoltaic modules on the roof producing 200 kilowatts of electricity for the facility and is the seventh Frito-Lay distribution center that produces electricity on-site with photovoltaic systems. The Modesto, CA SunChips production center has installed solar-heating concentrators and collectors on the grounds, and this center uses the solar super-heated hot water to heat the facility's cooking oil. In the last ten years, Frito-Lay has saved over $40 million in energy savings from energy-efficiency improvements that cut electrical consumption by 22% and fuel consumption by 24%. Since 1999, this company has decreased its overall water consumption by 35% (1 billion gallons saved) by adapting various water-reclamation techniques in production processes nationwide.

Burgerville, Vancouver, WA — Fast Food Restaurants

This Pacific Northwest fast-food company has 39 restaurants and 1,500 employees scattered throughout the states of Oregon and Washington. All of the energy consumed at the eateries and the corporate headquarters facility is offset by a corresponding amount of wind-power energy credits from a number of Washington locations. One of the most impressive accomplishments is an ongoing food-waste composting operation at each of the 39 restaurants, with the rich compost returned to farms and gardens in the area.

This organization has developed an impressive list of regional food sources that supply the major part of its menu items. Beef is sourced from a co-op of family ranches near Antelope, OR, with no growth hormones or antibiotics given to the cattle. This regional year-round arrangement allows the company to serve meat that has never been frozen and to reduce food transportation costs. Buns and breads are baked by a large family-owned bakery, eliminating the need for preservatives and again minimizing food transportation costs. All cheese, sourced from a century-old co-op of small dairy farms, is free of hormones and antibiotics. These dairy ranchers all fence cattle from sensitive riparian corridors along streams and rivers and protect the integrity of salmon habitats. Premium Walla Walla sweet yellow onions are procured from the rolling hills in the Walla Walla area of southeastern Washington, while blackberries used in pies and other desserts come from the Willamette Valley of northwestern Oregon. The firm commitment of Burgerville to regionally locate all 39 company restaurants and to source nearly all food products inside Washington and Oregon not only provides high quality delicious food but also supports the region's farmers and ranchers, circulates wealth within the region, and contributes to a durable economic base.

All employees that work a minimum of 20 hours per week for six months are eligible for employer-subsidized health insurance at a cost of $15 per month. This rare opportunity for affordable health coverage in the fast-food industry costs Burgerville $3 million per year, but has lowered new employee training costs by decreasing worker turnover rate to one-third of pre-program levels and has built an unusually loyal and productive work force. Burgerville prominently publicizes company sustainable business innovations at each restaurant location, and this company has enjoyed double-digit restaurant sales increases during the recent period of change and improvement.

Metro Health Hospital and Village, Wyoming, MI — Full Service Health Care Facility

In October 2007, the new 208-bed osteopathic Metro Health Hospital opened inside the 170-acre suburban Metro Health Village. A deed restriction requires all buildings of the village to be LEED™ certified; examples of tenant businesses include an adult day-care center, medical fitness center, physician offices, medical suppliers, and restaurants. One of only a handful of LEED-certified hospitals in the world, Metro Health has a number of distinguishing facility characteristics: a one-plus acre vegetated roof visible from most patient rooms, a parking lot storm runoff system filtered by a series of rain gardens, low-flow faucets and urinals, energy-saving motion-sensor interior lighting, adjustable lighting inside patient rooms, low-VOC (volatile organic compound, which is harmful to respiratory systems) interior paint and furniture, eye-soothing curved-path hallways illuminated by ambient light, a healing garden, jogging paths, and a playground.

Metro hired a sustainable practices officer two years before moving to the new hospital facility and continues to rely upon this officer to lead further innovation in internal hospital processes and procedures. In the heavily regulated health-care environment, the sustainable practices officer, along with numerous innovation team members, have arranged for the use of Green Seal™ Certified cleaning products, biodegradable cafeteria plates and utensils, and microfiber floor mops that use 90% fewer cleaning chemicals and save tens of thousands of gallons of water per year. An intern from a sustainable business program at a local college contributed to the efforts by developing an on-line carpooling program available for all Metro Health Village employees.

Green Mountain Coffee Roasters, Waterbury, VT — Coffee, Tea, and Cocoa Processor and Distributor

Located in northern Vermont, this publically held company employs a staff of over 900 and topped $500 million in revenue in 2007. Green Mountain markets over 100 selections of coffee, tea, and cocoa as well as single-cup brewing systems. Green Mountain reduces the negative effects of its energy choices by investing in efficient bean-packaging machinery and lighting systems in its central production facility as well as purchasing enough renewable energy certificates from Native Energy, LLC and Clean Air-Cool Planet to rightly claim carbon neutrality in its own production operation. Some material innovations include selling only coffee filters that are dioxin-free and whitened with an oxygen process, offering the industry's first biodegradable bulk-purchase coffee bean bag, and producing a compostable, carbon-neutral to-go beverage container made of paper from sustainably harvested forests.

Five percent of Green Mountain profits are donated back to communities that grow its coffee and are used in a variety of projects and locations. The company also partnered with Wild Oats Markets, Inc. and NPO Coffee Kids to develop an organic community garden operation for producers of Green Mountain's Fair Trade Xanica coffee in Mexico, which lacked a thoughtfully produced, nutritious local food source.

Green Mountain offers each employee up to 52 hours per year of paid time to volunteer for a community-based project of choice. Other benefits provided to each Green Mountain employee include a 90%-paid health-care policy, 20 hours of advancement training, a minimum "Vermont living wage" of $10.74 per hour, and access to an on-site massage therapist during peak production periods.

Wainwright Bank, Boston, MA — Commercial Bank

This publicly held commercial bank that employs 155 full-time employees tallied over $600 million in deposits and loans and claimed $6 million in net income in 2007. The Wainwright Bank Green Loan™ program was begun in 2001 and finances residential solar and wind energy, septic systems, replacement windows, and insulation projects. In order to reduce vehicle use, the company offers online banking and bill payment, no drive-up facilities (eliminates the pollution from idling vehicles in line), the ability for commercial customers to remotely scan and deposit checks, and public transportation subsidies for bank employees. In addition, loans for hybrid vehicles are offered at a 0.5% discount from the conventional vehicle loan rate.

The commitment to diversity in staff and client services is demonstrated by the 22 foreign languages spoken by Wainwright employees. Spousal insurance benefits are extended to all domestic partners of employees, and financial planning seminars for women are offered to encourage economic independence. The bank has committed over $75 million to finance well-built and affordable housing for low-income community members including the elderly, physically challenged, and mentally handicapped.

Wainwright Bank has made available millions of dollars in community development loans to non-profit organizations that are dedicated to environmental and sustainable causes, including *The Trust for Public Land, Silent Spring Institute, Union of Concerned Scientists,* and *Earthwatch Institute.* Over 30 other local and national non-profit organizations have chosen to bank with Wainwright. A three-year competitive-rate CD is offered to customers that also functions as a line-of-credit collateral for the Equal Exchange, a fair trade coffee, tea, and cacao merchant that has helped establish over 30 farmer co-ops in 16 developing nations. The bank routinely distributes promotional materials to its local bank customers on such items as compact fluorescent light bulbs, wildflower seeds, and reusable shopping bags. Furthermore, two Wainwright Bank branch offices are LEED-certified.

Bazzani Associates, Grand Rapids, MI — Commercial Real Estate Development

Founded in 1981 by sole proprietor Guy Bazzani, this real estate development and construction company began to embed TTL values into its mission at the start of the new millennium. At that time, Bazzani recognized the opportunity to specialize in sustainable commercial facility development and has enjoyed increased economic, environmental, and social benefits from the change. Two examples typical of the company's successful and award-winning building projects include the following:

- The adaptive renovation of a historic commercial structure that serves as the company headquarters and includes a vegetative roof, combined efficiency improvements that lower utility rates by 40%, features conducive to particularly high indoor air quality, and a LEED™ silver rating.

- The reclamation of a brown field site (a former industrial location with a significant amount of pollution remaining on-site) into a four-unit commercial facility with a vegetative roof and a land-scaped rain garden, which eliminates storm-water discharge; passive heating and lighting features; and high energy-efficiency design characteristics throughout.

The company routinely involves the neighboring community in project decisions and works to garner local support for the particular components of each project. Bazzani employees are also given paid time off to serve sustainable non-profit organizations, such as Local First of West Michigan, which advances development and patronization of locally owned businesses in the region.

Interface, Inc., Atlanta, GA — Soft-Surface Floor Covering Manufacturer

Ray Anderson founded Interface in 1973 and today, 50-plus acquisitions later, the company has become the world's largest manufacturer of modular commercial carpeting and a leader in the production of broadloom carpeting, panel fabrics, and upholstery fabrics. The company owns manufacturing facilities on four continents, has offices in over 100 countries, and has seen profits increase from $191 million in 2003 to $378 million in 2007.

Interface has saved over $370 million since 1995 by eliminating over two-thirds of its waste stream. The portion of reprocessed and bio-based materials used to manufacture products grew to 25% in 2007. Interface diverted 18 million pounds of refuse carpet from landfills in 2006, with 84% of this material reprocessed into new carpeting, 14% combusted for energy production, and 2% repurposed into new materials. Interface now uses renewable energy sources for over 27% of its current power demands and has reduced greenhouse gas emissions from its production processes by one-third since 1996.

The company offers low-VOC carpet brands for home or office such as Flor™ and Bentley Prince Street™; when customers are ready to replace this carpet, Interface picks up the old carpet free of charge and reprocesses it into new carpeting. With its commercial Interface Flor™ brand, the company offers an option of using a VOC-free tile installation with TacTiles™, small squares of PET (polyethylene terephthalate; a low toxicity polyester polymer) that reduce adverse toxic effects by 90% compared to conventional carpet adhesives.

Interface also values and keeps track of a number of employee metrics such as the average hours of training per employee per year, the percentage of females in management, and the number of employee family events held in all company locations. In 2007, Interface employees volunteered over 15,000 hours of work for various community organizations.

Shaw Industries Group, Inc., Dalton, GA — Full-Service Flooring Manufacturing

Shaw began as a publically traded corporation in 1971 and has grown to a company with $5 billion in sales and 30,000 employees worldwide. This flooring producer has also taken some large steps toward offering a product-of-service floor covering. Shaw carpet components include a pile fiber called EcoSolutionQ® and a carpet backing called EcoWorx® that are both part of a take-back system that reprocesses each type of worn-out materials into the same carpet fiber and backing with the same material integrity as the first-generation product. As a part of this free nationwide collection program located in 42 cities, the company delivers the fiber to a recovery center in Augusta, GA where the worn-out materials are processed back into more EcoSolutionQ carpet fiber, and the carpet backing to a recovery center in Cartersville, GA, where it is cycled back into more

EcoWorx® backing. This combination of fiber and backing cycling provides dozens of different textures, patterns, and colors of performance broadloom carpeting for Shaw.

Other innovations include installing a heat exchanger to recover waste-water heat for reuse at eight Shaw operations sites, contributing considerable energy savings; a 98% reduction of carpet shipping materials by replacing two-part boxes with cardboard sleeves and a shrink-wrap outer covering; and a program for Shaw's Information Technology Services and Customer Services that allows employees to work remotely from home, saving transportation fuel, emissions, and time spent commuting.

Herman Miller, Inc., Zeeland, MI — Commercial Office Furniture Manufacturer

This publicly held global provider of office furniture began its tenure in 1923 in Zeeland, MI and has grown to over $2 billion in sales in 2008. HMI has a long history of environmental concern as evidenced by the policy of using only sustainably harvested hardwoods in its products since 1991 and becoming a founding member of the United States Green Building Council in 1993, the parent organization of the popular LEED building program. The company's beautiful and effective GreenHouse assembly plant building in Holland, MI was awarded the LEED Pioneer building status in 1995 for functioning as a pilot project for the development of the LEED rating system. Among other rewards, the facility has 30% lower utility costs and twice the production of the similarly sized building that it replaced. Officials at Herman Miller have now set LEED silver ranking as the minimum criterion for all new construction projects and renovations.

Today the organization has new product designs evaluated and rated by the external industrial product and process firm McDonough Braungart Design Chemistry (MBDC) in three key areas: material chemistry toxicity, disassembly of the product, and the ability of materials to be reprocessed. Four models of Herman Miller chairs have received various levels of MBDC certification — the Celle, Mirra, Caper, and Embody — and all are PVC-free and quickly disassembled. Over 95% of the materials within them are able to be reprocessed and reused. An example of an MBDC-certified industrial process is the use of the GreenShield™ water and stain repellent for upholstery, which conditions a number of HMI furniture products.

Herman Miller satisfies 28% of its electrical demand today by renewable energy sources; has reduced its hazardous waste, solid waste, and VOC emissions by more than 80% of base year 1994; and is well on its way to a complete elimination goal for all three by the year 2020. The organization also authored its first annual comprehensive sustainability report in 2007 that is open to the public in its entirety. On the social front, Herman Miller employees volunteered over 33,000 hours to community-based causes in 2006 alone. Other social efforts include a company-wide contest for employees who lower their personal carbon emissions; employees with the strongest reduction efforts receive locally grown organic produce or gift certificates for local bike shops.

Steelcase Inc., Grand Rapids, MI — Commercial Office Furniture Manufacturer

The parent company of this commercial furniture giant was founded in 1912 and changed its name to Steelcase in 1958. This West Michigan company remained privately owned until 1998 and has led the global commercial furniture industry in product sales every year since 1974, with $3.4 billion in revenue garnered in 2008. The Grand Rapids, MI world headquarters campus now gets more than a quarter of its electricity from alternative sources with considerably more scheduled for the near future. One interesting sustainable-energy commitment for Steelcase in 2008 was a purchase of all the *renewable energy credits* (a tradable U.S. commodity of one megawatt-hour of electricity that was generated from a renewable source) for at least the first five years from a start-up 10-megawatt wind farm in the Texas Panhandle. Enough electricity will be sold locally from this wind farm to provide clean power for over 2,900 houses, thereby preventing 30,000 tons of carbon dioxide from entering the atmosphere per year.

Steelcase eliminated all VOC emissions from its metal finishing operations in 2003, and the company is targeting its 100-year anniversary in 2012 for company-wide elimination of VOCs. Since

1991, the company has reduced its global hazardous-waste production by 99%. Through a combination of technological upgrades, efficiency improvements, and reuse processes, the company cut global water consumption by 37% in just four years from 2003. Another noteworthy accomplishment in 2007 was the cycling of 22,000 tons of steel throughout the entire organization.

Completed in 2001, the LEED-certified wood-finishing facility in Grand Rapids enjoys ample daylight from large windows, computer/light-sensor-controlled interior lighting, lead-free water pipes, and three water-retention ponds that make available up to 700,000 gallons of water for landscape irrigation. An additional 1 million gallons of water are saved through a system of low-flow toilets and faucets inside the plant. The facility also offers convenient bike racks, locker rooms, and showers for employees who commute via bicycles to and from work.

Examples of innovative, high-performance products include the industry's first compostable fabric, Climatex® Lifecycle™, and the first office furniture certified by MBDC, the Think® chair, plus 26 other products or workstations that are MBDC certified.

In 1951, the company established the Steelcase Foundation for the purpose of independently awarding grants inside the communities where Steelcase employees live and work. In 2007, the organization provided over $8.3 million in grants and matching gifts to various non-profit organizations that focus on community development, the environment, education, and the arts. The foundation awarded Aquinas College of Grand Rapids, MI a $1 million grant in 2005 to promote and develop its fledgling Sustainable Business Program, which includes the first Bachelor of Science degree available in the U.S.

4.2 European For-Profit Companies

Allianz SE, Munich, Germany — Insurance, Banking, Asset Management

With its beginnings in 1890, this global company now employs more than 180,000 workers and had $136 billion in total revenue in 2007.

A core working group implements and manages sustainable business initiatives while reporting directly to the Board of Management and International Executive Committee. The company cultivates innovation with its "Ideas to Success" program, and over 60,000 ideas have been submitted by employees, with some of the company's greatest achievements coming from the front lines. For example, the idea to offer low-premium accident *micro-insurance* (low coverage with low premiums sold to low-income people) to nations like Colombia, using supermarkets as the intermediary, was an employee-submitted suggestion. To date, over 640,000 policies have been sold to many Colombians who had never been offered the opportunity for such an arrangement. In addition, death and disability, life, accident, and health micro-insurance are offered inside India, Indonesia, Egypt, and Senegal using various non-governmental organizations to broker the sales.

From 2006 to 2008, Allianz was the leading direct insurer on the Dow Jones Sustainability Index. The company now uses the G3 sustainability indicators (provided by the international non-profit organization Global Reporting Initiative) and has benchmarked its progress in economic, environmental, and social areas. Allianz has a standing requirement for all of its suppliers to pay a living wage, to abide by legal working hours and conditions, to eschew child labor or forced labor, and to have programs in place to minimize pollution, energy consumption, and materials exploitation. Included in a list of seven sustainable business products and services are a green-bond-fund offering that invests in renewable energy and energy efficiency companies, an EU carbon fund that trades carbon-emission allowances, and wind-energy investment opportunities.

Allianz promotes from within while using an intranet system to advertise opportunities for advancement and a global talent-management system that matches talents and career objectives with company needs. The company also retains active memberships in various sustainably focused external organizations including The Working Group on Principles for Sustainable Insurance, Transparency International, UN Global Compact, and Germany's Forum on Sustainability.

Co-operative Financial Services, Manchester, United Kingdom — Consumer Cooperative

Founded in 2002, Co-operative Financial Services (CFS) includes a member-owned-and-operated commercial bank, a full-service Internet bank, insurance company, and investment firm that are part of the larger Co-operative Group, the largest consumer cooperative in the U.K., with over 6.5 million members. This organization features a wide variety of TTL value-producing initiatives led by customers in its day-to-day operations. The 25-story tower company headquarters in Manchester, UK has been equipped on three sides with over 7,200 vertically mounted photovoltaic panels as well as 24 roof-mounted wind turbines that generate 180,000 kilowatts and 56,000 kilowatts of electricity per year respectively. A peregrine falcon nesting box was also installed on the roof with a real-time camera mounted so that people can watch and learn about these beautiful birds that sometimes share urban skyscraper locales with humans. More than 87% of company written materials in 2007 were printed on totally chlorine-free paper with vegetable-based inks and waterless printing.

Perhaps even more impressive are some of the business practices instigated at CFS. Each year, members vote online to direct policies such as denying loans to companies that extensively pollute, exploit animals, or take advantage of struggling third-world nations. The organization offers special credit cards, through which CFS purchases and protects half an acre of Brazilian rainforest the first time the card is used and continue to donate 0.25% of all purchase amounts to protecting rainforest habitat. The holder of this credit card enjoys competitive basic terms and interest rates and also receives a 5% lower interest rate on all purchases made from selected businesses that demonstrate TTL practices. Similarly, the organization offers another credit card through which it makes donations to organizations like Amnesty International and Oxfam when the account is opened. All credit cards issued by Co-operative Financial Services are not made from PVC but rather from polyethylene-terephthalate, which is a chlorinated hydrocarbon-free plastic material.

The Cooperative Bank branch has set aside a $50 million special fund to use for microloans to support small independent businesses in the world's poorest nations. A second special fund is available for locally based community development providers in the UK, and this loan is restricted to entrepreneurs disadvantaged in age, ability, or ethnicity.

CFS is especially supportive to the incarcerated population in the UK. The cooperative currently offers a pilot basic financial course in six prisons and intends to expand the program. CFS also sponsors an annual show of prisoner art works and uses sales revenue to re-invest in various rehabilitation projects for the prisoners.

The Co-operative Insurance branch offers discounted auto insurance policies for members who own high-mileage or electric vehicles. The organization provides access to a library of helpful information on pregnancy for all pregnant employees, and it provides the booklet "A Guide to a Working Pregnancy for Managers" to all organization administrators. A special rest and relaxation facility for pregnant women employees was opened at CFS headquarters in 2007. The organization has also adapted a sustainable procurement strategy policy and releases an annual comprehensive sustainability report.

Switcher SA, Lausanne, Switzerland — Garment Manufacturer

Switcher is a small Swiss corporation founded in 1981 that manufactures and sells low-priced casual clothing items made from high-quality materials. The organization outsources much of its manufacturing processes but closely monitors and attempts to influence the production standards of its supply chain. All cotton suppliers are required to provide stock that contains only trace levels of heavy metals, pesticides, VOCs, and carcinogens. Every Switcher supplier must agree to an initial environmental and social performance audit and to work with Switcher to improve its production standards. All garment shipping boxes are bleached with a chlorine-free process, and the ink printed on the containers is free of heavy metals.

The company donated roof space atop its headquarters facility in Lausanne to Edisun Power Company for the installation of a 600-square-meter photovoltaic system that averages 10,000 kilowatt hours per month production for the customers of the utility. At a Switcher T-shirt supply-chain facility in Tirupur, India, textile mills are powered by seven wind turbines, and cafeteria meals for employees are cooked in a solar oven. The company co-financed a community water cycling plant here and subsequently reduced water consumption by 95%.

Corporate managers at Switcher are held accountable for respectful treatment of all workers and for encouraging effective, free-flowing communication throughout the entire company. The organization offers four months of maternity leave for its female workers and the employee option of a part-time work schedule upon return. Employees at some of its developing world supply facilities are provided the opportunity to attend various educational classes, including environmental educational courses.

Precious Woods, Zurich, Switzerland — Sustainable Timber Harvesting

This publicly traded company with over $80 million in revenue in 2007 and 1,600 employees, specializes in sustainably harvested timber operations. Precious Woods has international operations in Costa Rica, Brazil, Nicaragua, the Democratic Republic of Congo, Gabon, and the Netherlands. The company adheres to the Forest Stewardship Council guidelines for harvest practices and processes nearly all hardwood materials in the locality of the extraction, employing mostly local workers. As part of its sustainable forestry strategy, the company leaves at least 20% of the harvestable timber uncut and never harvests along waterways or steep slopes, thus reducing adverse soil erosion effects. The company typically uses directional tree felling to minimize damage to uncut neighboring trees and takes care to prevent damage to the forest floor by using light equipment and cables to drag the logs to the skid trail where mobile loaders transport the timber to awaiting trucks.

Employees who harvest field timber in developing nations are provided with training and education programs that include communication skills, equipment safety procedures, disease prevention, first aid, and alcohol abuse. Precious Woods avoids timber harvest in areas inhabited by nomadic indigenous peoples and allows sedentary local peoples to continue to use company land in their customary ways.

Abengoa, Seville, Spain — Sustainability Technology in Energy and Infrastructure

This publicly held parent company is organized into five separate units: solar, bio-energy, environmental services, information technology, and industrial engineering and construction. With nearly 14,000 employees and $4 billion in revenue in 2007, company operations include the design, construction, and operation of various types of solar technology and fuel cells. Solar power projects have been completed at multiple locations in Spain, the U.S., China, Algeria as well as Morocco that include concentrated solar power for large-scale commercial power plants and conventional and thin-film photovoltaic technology for smaller-scale applications. An example of other tangential technological developments is an on-board bus-fare collection system that uses magnetic strip swipe cards that allow quick and accurate fare crediting for passengers.

Abengoa offers on-site day care, fitness, and medical centers as well as maternity leave and flextime for most of its employees. In Seville, Spain where company headquarters are located, the Focus Abengoa Foundation operates inside the Los Venerables Hospital while also providing continual financial and administrative assistance to the community health-care provider. From this location, the company supports a variety of international community building programs including a four-decade-old collaborative program with a religious organization in Argentina, which operates three local community centers providing food, medicine, and job training for the poor, disabled, orphaned, or uneducated and school improvements in poverty-stricken areas of Argentina and Peru, making available clean water, electricity, and well-equipped kitchens.

4.3   Caribbean and South American For-Profit Companies

Tiamo Resort, South Andros Island, Bahamas —
Sustainable Tourist Resort

This vacation destination provides a distinct departure from the typical Caribbean experience. Accommodations are limited to 11 private beach bungalows with screened-in porches offering a panoramic view of the pristine natural surroundings and providing shade for the main living areas and maximized cooling airflow. Within walking distance of each bungalow one can snorkel and dive through a huge world-class coral reef. During construction of the resort, site clearing was completed by hand, with special care taken to protect surrounding vegetation, and the orientation of each bungalow was determined by the natural topography and characteristics of the building site. The construction crew consisted of 20 local craftsmen, with only three non-Bahamians as part of the team. Energy for small power tools used during construction and for the continuous operation of the resort has been powered by an on-site series of photovoltaic panels and a battery storage system. Solar water heaters also supply all the hot water used in each bungalow and in the administrative complex. Human waste is processed by low-flush composting toilets, all *grey water* (from sinks and washing machines) is treated with sand and gravel filters, and all food waste is composted and used as garden fertilizer. Tiamo uses simple cleaning mixtures of baking soda and vinegar in place of harsh chemical mixtures and purchases as many resort supplies as possible from local businesses. Continual improvement at the resort is aided by guests who are encouraged to offer suggestions that would further improve the day-to-day TTL operations.

All Tiamo staff members share the commitment of the organization for its guests, the natural world, and the nearby human communities. Visitors are given an introductory tour of the resort's sustainability practices and later have the opportunity to attend field trips with naturalists who explain the ecology of the area. The resort staff regularly work with local schools to help educate students about the natural environment. Tiamo has also partnered with a variety of

ed. systems

world environmental organizations such as Reef Relief, The Wildlife Conservation Society, Shedd Aquarium (Chicago), and The Bahamas National Trust to further develop other educational initiatives.

The Black Sheep Inn, Cotopaxi, Ecuador — Sustainable Tourist Resort

This resort is located above 10,000 feet in the Andes Mountains, approximately 60 miles southwest of the capital city of Quito, Ecuador. Resort guests that arrive by bicycle receive a 10%–15% discount, depending on the length of stay. A 10-acre organic garden provides food for the guests and is supported by a passive solar-heated greenhouse and an attached chicken house that provides effective night heating with the dissipated body heat of roosting chickens. A variety of insect-repelling plants are used in the garden to safely keep crop pests at bay. Domestically raised animals include egg-laying ducks, geese, and chickens; llamas; and the famous black sheep. All resort food waste is either fed to the animals or composted and used for garden fertilizer. An electric water pump powered by two photovoltaic panels provides the power to move pond water for garden irrigation, a decorative fountain, and a waterslide. The Inn exclusively uses composting toilets set inside bathrooms with clear roofs and large windows that provide spectacular views of the Andes Mountains. Each bathroom is filled with small flower and vegetable gardens that are fertilized with the composted waste provided by resort guests. Laundry is done by hand with rainwater collected in roof cisterns and is line dried.

A small public library has been established by employee and guest donations for the nearby community with eight computers and over 1,000 books. The Black Sheep Inn has subsidized local school textbook purchases since 2002. The resort has supported local entrepreneurship by providing an interest-free loan that allowed a nearby family to open a horseback riding business for resort visitors. The Inn sells a variety of woven garments with all proceeds going directly to the local artisans. Furthermore, the Inn has co-sponsored a variety of community workshops with the U.S. Peace Corps in the areas of nutrition, public health, family planning, naturalist skills, and weaving.

4.4 Australian For-Profit Companies

Australian Gas Light Energy Limited, North Sydney, New South Wales — Electric Utility

This power company offers customers the opportunity to choose a percentage of "green power" (solar, wind, landfill methane, and biomass) they would like to buy throughout the year at a 5.5c per kWh premium. Customers may also opt for short-term 100% green power events, which provide unique educational opportunities about alternative energy choices. The utility uses a diverse energy-source profile including coal, methane, hydroelectric, wind, solar, and cogeneration with macadamia nuts. Nut shells are burned to super-heat boiler water, 20% of which is used to process a local company's macadamia nut output, and the remaining 80% is used to generate electricity for the utility.

At company's headquarters in Sydney, the company uses solar-controlled window blinds and efficient heating, lighting, and ventilation systems to supplement its diverse power-source portfolio. Australian Gas Light Energy Limited is listed on the Dow Jones Sustainability World Index and publishes an annual sustainability report. The utility helps to build social capital by funding energy use in four homeless shelters, by matching all employee charitable contributions, and by partnering with Mission Australia, a non-profit organization that offers support services to the homeless Australians.

4.5 Asian For-Profit Companies

East Japan Railway Company, Tokyo, Japan — Rail Mass Transit

This major publically held Japanese transit company, which had revenues of $27 billion in fiscal year 2008, serves over 16 million passengers daily with 53,000 employees. The company has pioneered the use of diesel/electric hybrid rail cars and is using fuel-cell powered electric trains on a limited trial basis. Photovoltaic panels are employed to provide a portion of the electricity for rail stations in

Tokyo and Takaki, the general training center and the research and development facility of the company. Plastic fare cards with activated magnetic strips have replaced over 20 million paper tickets annually. These cards require a refundable deposit and, consequently, are nearly always returned for reuse. Hundreds of thousands of employee uniforms are made from the reprocessed plastic polymer *polyethylene terephthalate*, providing a second generation use for this food and beverage container material. The company reclaims all of its food waste in its Tokyo train stations, composts the material, and sells the humus to local farmers and gardeners. More than 20 vegetative roofs have been installed on various company buildings, which cover more than 7,000 square meters throughout Japan.

The recent installation of sound-deadening walls and continuously welded rail tracks has reduced noise levels along selected routes by nearly two-thirds. The transit company has promoted local ecotourism in Japan via its "Hiking from Stations" program through which it organized over 400 nature hikes with nearly 200,000 participants in 2008. To increase the comfort level and safety of female passengers, East Japan Railway has introduced "women only" cars for late-night trips and morning rush-hour commuters. The company has also worked closely with local governments and childcare businesses to establish daycare centers for children near train stations for commuting workers. For employees that care for elderly family members (a common practice in Japan), adult daycare centers have been established at four different railroad company offices. The company has published and made available a yearly sustainability report since 2002.

Aeon Corporation, Chiba, Japan — Large-Scale, Multi-Product Retail Centers

The roots of this publicly traded Japanese conglomerate extend back to the mid-18th century. Today, Aeon consists of a group of 169 companies that build and operate shopping centers in Asia with member supermarkets, drugstores, home centers, convenience stores, specialty stores, financial services, entertainment establishments, and restaurants. Revenues in 2007 were over $46 billion.

Aeon tailors the composition of each retail center to the needs and tastes of each particular location.

Nearly all stores built in 2009 have photovoltaic systems that generate a percentage of the electrical demand for the facility. These new "ecostores" also have incorporated a number of other positive innovations. Food waste is commonly diverted from the landfill stream and is composted. To encourage customers to bring and use durable shopping bags, Aeon retail stores charge for thin plastic shopping bags and donate the proceeds to various community environmental causes. On select days, Aeon stores donate 1% of all purchases made by customers with their own shopping bags to various community projects. The company employs reusable packing crates in its food-operation businesses and displays clothing items on durable, in-store hangers. Some product packaging and store shopping baskets are made from bio-based materials. Aeon was the first Japanese general retailer to sign the Ministry of the Environment-sponsored commitment to help establish a cycling-based material society in Japan.

Employees are allowed to modify their working schedules to align with the various stages in their lives. To accommodate home care demands for young children and elderly family members, Aeon will reduce the amount of working hours of the employee according to their requests. Employees with children attending elementary school are never transferred to distant work locations until after the children have completed the current school year. Employee promotions from within the company are commonplace, with a series of in-house business training sessions available to all employees throughout their careers. Aeon has also partnered with the international non-profit organization UNICEF to help build 149 schools in Cambodia and 57 schools in Nepal.

Sharp Corporation, Tokyo, Japan — Electronic Communication and Information Equipment and Components, and Home Appliances

Founded in 1912 and incorporated in 1935, Sharp generated over $34 billion in revenues in 2007 and currently employs nearly

61,000 employees worldwide with a manufacturing operation that includes a wide variety of electronics devices and home appliances. Sharp has been the world's largest producer of photovoltaic systems from 2001 to 2008 and has also employed this energy technology inside some of its own facilities. The Kameyama complex in the western part of the Japanese large island of Honshu has over 47,000 square meters of photovoltaic equipment that generates over 5,200 kW of electricity (energy equivalent to service 1,300 homes). The liquid crystal display (LCD) plant and the distribution center have PV panels mounted on their roofs and outside walls; a third production facility has cutting-edge transparent thin PV film mounted on the south-facing windows. The complex also has four 250 kW fuel cells, which complement the PV system by contributing electricity to the complex at night and on cloudy days.

On the industrial materials front, Sharp has made a number of technological advances that allow the reclamation, reprocessing, and re-use of a variety of product components. The company now separates and recovers the plastic polymer polypropylene from the waste stream, the soft metal indium from non-functioning LCD panels, and the silicon from old PV cells and reprocesses these materials into high-quality new components. Sharp is collaborating with five other electronics companies to operate 190 pick-up sites and 18 reprocessing facilities for non-functioning household appliances in Japan. The company also takes back, disassembles, and reprocesses outdated and non-functioning personal computers, office copy machines, and toner cartridges.

All Sharp employees receive one of three levels of environmental education based on their duties: the basic level includes current environmental issues; the expert level includes environmental policy and design-for-cycling topics; and the master level includes a comprehensive understanding of sustainable technology and products. Throughout the tenure of an employee, he/she is assisted in writing a professional development plan and in improving technological skills through in-house training. Sharp workers have the opportunity to participate in voluntary physical fitness, nutrition, and mental health programs. Sharp supports neighboring communities near its facilities by sponsoring local festivals and major tree reforesting projects and by opening company recreational facilities — tennis courts, gymnasiums, and ball fields — to the public.

4.6 Non-Profit Organizations

Formal associations that exist in the U.S. for the purpose of supporting charitable, educational, religious, and other public service efforts are often incorporated and hold 501(c)(3) tax-exempt status. This type of non-profit organization (NPO) is staffed by volunteers, paid staff, or a combination of both working to provide programs and services that benefit the public good but that are not made available by existing for-profit companies. The NPO usually has individual members or entire organizations as members in contrast to the for-profit business that has individuals or entire companies as customers. Membership is motivated by a perceived benefit from the association with the NPO and often requires payment of annual dues. Major policies and activities within these organizations are usually governed by a board of directors that is nominated and voted in by members and voted upon by the members. Some recognizable examples of non-profit organizations are Goodwill Industries, United Way, Habitat for Humanity, Red Cross, Better Business Bureau, and Amnesty International.

Sustainable business practices are certainly applicable and advantageous for NPOs, which essentially are service groups that concentrate on providing value for their membership. The voluntary nature of non-profit work often fosters an egalitarian atmosphere among NPO staff and provides an opportunity to establish a flat organizational structure with workers who are most closely involved in each issue and in making decisions. Sharing of information may also be expedited and expanded in flatly organized institutions, increasing the ability of the NPO to effectively respond to changing circumstances while empowering both salaried and volunteer employees. Open and transparent day-to-day operations, along with purposeful sharing of information throughout the organization, cultivates buy-in and meaningful contributions from all parts of the constituency group.

The emphasis in sustainable business on recognizing inter-relationships among groups of people, the natural world, and commerce and the subsequent developing of collaborative social processes that positively reinforces these relationships offer two important lessons for non-profit organization leaders. First, the opportunity exists for refining the ambitions of the NPO into more effective and valuable goals. For example, rather than a Chamber of Commerce concentrating on attracting foreign corporations with various incentives, this agency could recalibrate its goals to include promoting locally owned and controlled businesses that have a track record of setting down deep roots in a single community. Similarly, rather than an environmental-activist NPO perpetuating an adversarial relationship with business, the NPO could instead redesign its efforts toward finding win-win situations for combined environmental and business causes.

The second critical challenge for metropolitan NPOs is to actively coordinate community service efforts, avoiding overlapping initiatives, and to seek partnerships that leverage the strength of each institution for the greater good. An effective first step is to bring together all regional NPO leaders for the purpose of establishing a community mapping document that displays all the NPOs along with their roles. If significant overlaps exist among institutions, a mutually agreed upon division of responsibilities is negotiated, or mergers of two or more NPOs may even be arranged. When non-profit organization officials recognize and appreciate the advantages of regular communication and cooperation, as well as the handicap of operating in isolation, then the collective potential of collaborative community endeavors will emerge much more powerful than the sum of its parts.

Although often a less consequential part of the operation, non-profit organization leaders can also explore building, energy, materials, and service provider options. Choices of where to set up shop (LEED-certified) and where to bank (locally owned and operated) as well as the type of promotional materials, office equipment, and energy use all provide opportunities to commit the NPO to a transition to sustainable business practices. Enlisting a community member with sustainable business proficiency as a board member or volunteer-at-large can help guide the selection of sustainable alternatives. A well-designed and well-maintained Website provides the vehicle for publicizing notable accomplishments and projects as well as natural- and human-world supporting activities. Taking on a sustainable persona will attract additional community interest and involvement for the NPO, while helping to lay the social foundations for life, happiness, and inter-generational opportunity.

4.7 Sustainable Business Forums

As leaders inside organizations are drawn to sustainable business and commit to the revolution, they are faced with the universal challenge of how to best convert company DNA into a sustainable institution. After reading an inspirational book, attending a conference, hiring a consultant to sharpen the company's transition vision, and identifying a few key employees who share their enthusiasm, change agents are often paused by the modicum of support during the challenging process. These individuals are well aware of the risk associated with significant change, so any knowledgeable assistance supporting their efforts is welcomed. This critical opportunity to provide peer-based support is sometimes filled by a not-for-profit regional business association commonly referred to as a sustainable business forum (SBF). As the name implies, SBF is an association of a group of organizations represented by committed individuals who come together with the common goal of advancing sustainable business practices in the region.

As a great restaurant district in a city benefits from a wide variety of blue-ribbon eating establishments, so does a locality benefit from a large number of organizations that are transitioning to sustainable practices. Sustainable business forums assist interested member organizations in learning about the principles and practices of the movement and guide new members in putting the theory into practice. SBF meetings provide the occasion for making contacts with other people who are helping guide their organization through meaningful change. Special events such as a speaker or a workshop covering a particular challenge of sustainable business are often sponsored by SBFs for their membership. Meetings also provide a networking opportunity for like-minded individuals who are facing similar reform challenges at their workplace.

As with most non-profit organizations, the composition of the board of directors is a critical factor in determining the effectiveness of the forum. One approach of existing SBFs that has successfully guided board composition is to include representation from small-sized locally owned businesses, medium-sized locally owned and incorporated businesses, and larger publicly-held corporations, as well as representation from both manufacturing and service-sector businesses, at least one economic-development NPO, one institution of higher education, and one level of government. Ideally, each board representative is a change leader for an institution that has made considerable transition progress or is atleast in the process of such sweeping changes. Board members generally function both as policy advisors and action committee leaders for special forum projects. For newly forming SBFs, a dedicated handful of passionate advocates is needed to patiently shepherd the organization through the inevitable early bumps in the road.

The adaptation of a mission statement is a standard part of the early formation efforts, and a vital component of this guiding declaration is a commitment to education. In both new and established SBFs, this component is often particularly challenging as the movement is still quite preliminary, splintered, and continuously evolving. Coming to a consensus about the vital parts of the movement among members of an education committee may even be difficult. At the very least, an agreement among board members concerning the definition of terms specific to sustainable business will lay the foundation for productive discussion and strategizing.

A service often requested by the forum membership is education about the movement. As mentioned earlier, this type of appeal is certainly understandable, considering the amount of misinformation and contradictory information in the media and the relatively early developmental stage of the campaign itself. In contrast to conventional business, the emerging field of sustainable endeavors is limited to generally chaotic and segregated messages from all but a few private sector visionaries. A clear and comprehensive educational program made available to membership via forum Web pages, portions of general meetings, and special events will provide the foundation for a more sophisticated, connected, and engaged membership. Finding a capable educator or team of educators for this task, however, is often quite a challenge for the forum leadership. At this early stage of the movement, it is quite rare to find someone locally with a combination of sustainable business knowledge and educational talent that has the ability to significantly advance the movement for organizations within the region. This situation may require the services of a qualified sustainable business consultant from outside the area. Settling for an under-qualified education facilitator is a sure way to present a potentially watered-down version of the movement to the membership and to stymie the regional growth of the movement.

Another program enthusiastically received by forum members is the sharing of "best sustainable practices" by representatives of particularly accomplished member organizations with the entire forum membership. This type of open mentoring offers rewards for both the presenting organization and the groups represented in the audience. Member representatives only recently involved in sustainable considerations hear first-hand how more experienced companies have successfully implemented change, and the presenting business representative demonstrates a leadership role in the movement. Although specific situations may vary considerably among the presenting company and audience, an explanation about how one organization approaches energy issues, material selection, or the tracking of a sustainable metrics system nearly always proves helpful to a variety of newcomers.

An opportunity exists for sustainable business forums to partner with other non-profit for the benefit of all organizations. Most metropolitan areas have quite a few functioning NPOs that deal with economic development, social issues, or environmental causes. As a rule, the staff inside these organizations tackle narrowly focused missions using volunteers and resources available inside each separate NPO. Rarely are steps taken to identify issues that are shared by other NPOs or to negotiate the combining of efforts of similarly motivated institutions. Non-profits are typically under-staffed and managers have difficulty finding the time required to build collaborative relationships. Unfortunately, as NPOs continue to focus inward, opportunities are lost that would offer long-term benefits otherwise unattainable for organizations operating in isolation.

The uncommon breadth of the sustainable business movement's TTL approach offers a clear opportunity for SBFs to partner with economic development, social equity, and environmental organizations. For example, existing NPOs that support locally owned businesses share this mission with most SBFs and their membership (even multinational corporation members use locally owned businesses to support operations). When an SBF partners with an NPO that is purpose-related NPO, each institution may benefit from the association by negotiated arrangements such as access to the other's membership for pertinent announcements, bulk purchasing for commonly purchased supplies, and co-sponsorship opportunities for presentations and seminars. Although this type of collaborative association has been uncommon in the past among NPOs, such agreements can deliver these and other substantial benefits that otherwise would not be possible.

In summary, the early role of a sustainable business forum is to facilitate fundamental movement education and provide networking opportunities for member organizations. When new members are asked by forum officials for program requests, the first priority is education sessions that will improve their understanding of sustainable business theory and their capability to apply those principles to their specific businesses. Longer-tenured forums later shift the focus to building collaborative relationships among member businesses and community non-profit organizations. Fully mature forum activities will include the pursuit of new sustainable practices and perhaps even the discovery of new components of the movement not previously uncovered.

West Michigan Sustainable Business Forum, Grand Rapids, MI

Established in 1994, the West Michigan Sustainable Business Forum (WMSBF) was one of the first forums on the scene in the U.S.

Anchored by the commercial furniture and vehicle parts industries, West Michigan has leveraged its deep-rooted heritage in environmental issues by forming an association that works to enhance the critical systems within a prosperous region. With only a handful of founding member companies, this potent forum has grown its membership to over 100 dues-paying organizations and has steadily advanced sustainable business practices in West Michigan for more than 15 years. Representatives attend monthly meetings hosted by various member businesses, with sustainable business education and best practice examples as part of each gathering. Once each year the WMSBF partners with three other younger Michigan SBFs to organize the annual Michigan SBF Conference, which features a schedule of speakers and numerous booths of sponsoring organizations that are active in the sustainable business movement in Michigan. The all-day event provides an opportunity for attendees to make contacts with other like-minded organization leaders and to improve their awareness of the most recent advances in the sustainable business movement.

4.8   Other U.S. Non-Profit Organizations

Rocky Mountain Institute, Old Snowmass, CO — Sustainable Living Systems Instruction

This NPO was founded in 1982 by L. Hunter and Amory Lovins and today employs 64 full-time staff members with an annual budget of $12 million. The RMI supports the sustainable business movement by demonstrating how business, communities, and government can take the TTL approach by making efficiency improvements in their operations. When the Institute designed and constructed its main facility in the early 1980s, it used the best energy-efficiency technology available, and 20 years later, it still demonstrates superior performance to most other comparable buildings. The structure is heated and illuminated in the day almost entirely by passive solar design, with a greenhouse in the center of the facility functioning as a humidifier. A photovoltaic system adjusts to most efficiently align itself with the height of the sun in the sky, and an active solar water-heating system further reduces conventional energy use. One of the primary building materials — stone — was gathered only half a mile from the construction site.

The RMI staff is a diverse collection of classically trained, accomplished professionals who are united in their commitment to respecting the values of others and to a systems-thinking approach that uses biological insights to find the best and least-expensive solution for each challenge they take on for their clients.

Sustainable Seattle, Seattle, WA — Regional Sustainable Practices Catalyst

Founded in 1991, this non-profit now manages an average annual budget of $250,000 that is made available through a variety of foundations and grants that support efforts to advance the long-term vitality of the Puget Sound Region. An eight-member board of directors currently made up of for-profit business people, NPO members, educators, government officials, and lawyers provides leadership and policy direction for the organization. Sustainable Seattle refocused the efforts of its five full-time staff members in 2008 to include three major initiatives: to develop strategic community sustainability projects, to build a network of sustainability practitioners addressing regional challenges, and to use previously crafted regional sustainability indicators to stimulate focused action. Each year, this NPO publishes an annual report that includes TTL performance metrics of the organization.

Business Alliance for Local Living Economies, San Francisco, CA — Local-Focused Economies Facilitator

This non-profit organization was founded in 2001 by authors David Korten and Michael Shuman and by business leaders Laury Hammel and Judy Wicks. Since that time, the Business Alliance for Local Living Economies has grown to over 60 local network affiliate organizations found in 26 states, the District of Columbia, and three Canadian provinces. The charge of the organization is to build community wealth by catalyzing and strengthening networks of locally owned businesses that are dedicated to building healthy economies by embedding sustainable agriculture, green buildings, renewable energy, zero waste manufacturing, and independent retail establishments into the community. A nine-person board of directors currently made up of graduate students, educators, NPO directors, and small- and medium-sized business owners also works to promote healthy workplaces and living wages in business and to protect the natural environment.

Colne Valley Regional Park, London, England — Urban Natural Area Advocate

This unique park is operated by a non-profit organization that was founded in 1965 with land donated by eight adjacent local governmental authorities. One full-time paid director coordinates a variety of volunteer community workers and government employees from the eight agencies that donated the original land for the project. A model for cross-jurisdictional collaboration, the park safeguards a 43-square-mile contiguous natural area of forest and wetlands, with trails throughout and an ongoing public outdoor education program. The $500,000 annual budget is funded by the eight local authority partners and includes wildlife population surveys, tree plantings, and pollution monitoring. The multiple-agency management of the regional park fosters continuous interaction and partnerships of private individuals and a variety of local authorities throughout the many counties, districts, and boroughs that make up the project.

California Academy of Sciences, San Francisco, CA — Scientific Research and Education

Founded over a century and a half ago, this international center for scientific education and research is headquartered in Golden Gate Park, San Francisco, CA inside a unique and multi-purpose structure. In addition to the administrative offices and research laboratories, the single building contains an aquarium, planetarium, natural history museum, four-story rainforest, 3-D theater, naturalist center, lecture hall, two restaurants, and 2.5-acre living roof populated with 1.7 million native plants. The building earned a platinum-level LEED certification from the U.S. Green Building Council.

Between 5% and 10% of the electricity (over 210,000 kilowatt hours per year) used by the building is generated by a walkway rooftop photovoltaic system. Other intelligent structural characteristics include the following: (1) skylights in the roof and floor-to-ceiling windows flood abundant natural light into the interior during the daytime; (2) hot water fills a comfortable and efficient radiant heating system in the floor; (3) a steep-sloped portion of the roof funnels cool air into an open-air plaza; (4) skylights and louvers open, providing ventilation for the building interior; (5) almost two-thirds of the building insulation is reprocessed blue jean denim cloth, a safer and more efficient insulating material than tradition fiberglass; (6) over 90% of the office space has natural lighting, ventilation, and windows that open; and (7) thirty-two thousand tons of sand from the foundation excavation were applied to Bay Area dune renovation projects.

The academy has also implemented numerous staff-friendly policies: (1) One-hundred percent of both medical and dental insurance is provided for all full-time employees; (2) Fifty percent of both medical and dental insurance is provided for all part-time employees, with both full- and part-time employees receiving no-cost life insurance for the one and one-half the value of the employee's annual salary; (3) all employees have access to an employee-assistance program, which provides confidential therapist consultations on various life issues and stress management; (4) employees may purchase Bay Area transit-system passes using pre-tax dollars; and (5) a subsidy is provided for those employees who walk, bike, carpool, or use public transportation to get to work.

4.9 Laying the Foundation

In the time it took to peruse this assortment of evolving organizations, at least one additional group of business leaders quite probably has committed to similar sustainable business ideals. During the time it took to bring this written text to bookstore shelves, the vast majority of organizations featured here have continued to make additional intrepid improvements, adding even more brick and mortar to the foundation of the movement. So many early participants exist all over the world that dozens of noteworthy pioneer organizations were not able to be included in this chapter. Indeed, an extensive array of sustainable business niches is appearing in various places today, with many openings not yet recognized by local entrepreneurs. Even so, in the next few years, an even richer assortment of ventures, establishments, and communities will strike off and break the conventional business mold and land profoundly in the bull's eye of opportunity, restoration, and durability. Hopefully, the examples in these pages will give you a considerable edge to understanding the implications of the movement and recognizing specific opportunities when they come your way.

Ironically, these first few years of cultural genesis have coalesced largely in spite of established formal educational process. Exploring "outside-the-box" solutions in business and rewarding on-target risk taking has not been a part of our mainstream contemporary process. Furthermore, when we do consider a solution that is outside the conventional box, leaders only rarely possess the required comprehensive knowledge to posit a systems approach that will benefit the entire community. An appreciation and understanding of the energy and material processes of natural systems is generally ignored in formal education. Many of the imaginative and successful movement ventures (as summarized in the previous section) have come from stimulating thought and experiences that, for the most part, were acquired outside of our formal education system, a system that has received copious financial private and public support. But that unfortunate reality can change. In the next chapter, we will examine the current focus of our education system and reconsider a felicitous role for educational institutions and scholars in our radical rearrangement of premises that guide the production of goods and services. We will re-envision what we teach and how we teach at all grade levels so as to best prepare future generations for the oppor-tunities that lie ahead.

Guide Point 4: The sustainable business movement has its roots well established throughout the worldwide business community in a wide fecund variety of forms.

Chapter 5

Greasing the Cognitive Skids

Consider the following statement: *A good person cannot do the right thing if he or she does not know what the right thing is.* Let us investigate the relevance of this simple declaration in the context of the sustainable business movement. If an ethical person is unaware of the serious pernicious effects caused by industry, would that person be likely to work to change that reality? If another ethical person realizes the extent of the problems but naively advocates ineffective symptomatic reform, would a meaningful solution be any closer? A reasonable answer to both questions is no. Today, not only are the people who are unaware of the extent of our unfortunate situation unable to remedy the root causes, but many well-intentioned advocates are advancing misguided answers. This unfortunate circumstance of limited base-line knowledge of both the problems and the solutions suggests an opportunity for educators to consider a *series of adjustments* in the content of existing formal education systems.

The first adjustment involves the acknowledgment of the myriad of irreplaceable and vital natural-world benefits and an understanding of how most conventional industry diminishes the capacity of natural systems to provide our needs. The second adjustment includes a familiarization with natural laws and their relevance for all communities on Earth. The third adjustment entails a clear understanding of the foundations of a redesigned industrial system that uses the sun as its energy source, cycles all materials in a healthy way, and positively contributes to all generations of all species. The fourth adjustment involves continual dialogue about improved TTL adaptive strategies within the parameters of the third adjustment for each business sector and business type.

The first two adjustments are well-suited for grades one to eight of formal education. The third adjustment is appropriate during the high school years, and the fourth adjustment fits best in college-level education. With the aforementioned four-part amendments integrated into our formal education process, profound systemic change will not only be possible, it will become inevitable. As thoughtful citizens develop and mature in the principles of sustainability, these added principles will drive positive change and result in a more advantaged human species over time. Short of these amendments to our current education framework, most of our developed-world citizens will fail to connect the insidious human-welfare catastrophes with the corresponding core causes. Those few who do somehow come to understand this reality will be limited in their ability to work toward an effective remedy for our hefty set of problems.

Incumbent upon leaders formal education is the adoption of newly discovered and well-supported sets of information into our overall body of knowledge, especially the relevant additions that improve our understanding of man's relationship with the natural world. Integrating a new set of perspectives as fundamentally challenging as those provided by sustainable business is not unprecedented. At various times after revolutionary discoveries were made, such as the spherical shape of the Earth by ancient Greeks and Persians that was later supported by Magellan and other Western explorers, the theory of evolution by Darwin and Wallace, and different perspectives on capitalism by Smith, Marx, and Friedman, the educational community integrated these new viewpoints with society's existing body of knowledge. The contribution of each major discovery provided the opportunity for practical application of the concomitant concepts into the day-to-day life for the benefit of the populace. International trade routes, the science of genetics, and versions of capitalism throughout recent history are examples of pragmatic applications of the above-cited revelations.

A persistent and expanding group of entrepreneurial pioneers is moving forward in this sustainable business revolution, and the educational institutions of the world must recognize the early successes of this organic movement that are standing up to public scrutiny.

Considering the relative urgency of specific sustainable business issues previously discussed such as global climate change, expediency in the corresponding educational revamp is also crucial. Formal education has the opportunity to significantly grease the cognitive skids of the movement by institutionalizing its authentic message and by effectively integrating the salient concepts within the generally accepted body of world knowledge and perspectives.

5.1 Connected on All Levels

In addition to augmenting school curricula with fundamental movement tenets, another value-added challenge for the educational community is to adopt an interdisciplinary approach at all levels of formal education. Identifying the subtle connections among academic disciplines and exploring these relationships in the classroom will better prepare a student to meaningfully contribute to the movement. The study of chemistry, for example, increases its usefulness when the inter-relationships with biology, physics, math, history, geography, sociology, environmental studies, art, and philosophy are considered. Each discipline, when examined within the context of all other fields of study, provides more educational currency than it would in isolation. The eminent Harvard biologist E.O. Wilson expounds this fundamental connectedness of all fields of study in his 1998 book *Consilience — The Unity of Knowledge.* Wilson posits that the world is orderly and can be explained by a few basic natural laws and, that in reality, the arts and sciences are closely related. He boldly and eloquently moves out of his biology expertise to make the case for the unity of all knowledge as a critical step for the salvation of humankind.

On a smaller scale, understanding natural processes, the humanities, and the connections between them is quite useful for change agents of companies that are committing to the movement. Predicting the overall effectiveness of an operational modification requires a thorough assessment of all consequences of that option. For example, manufacturing executives committed to the TTL approach might find themselves making a decision about whether their company will move from durable-product production/sales to a product-of-service operation. The ability of these leaders to make this assessment would significantly improve if they recognized the full implications and effects of this decision. Examples of these considerations include the following:

- The distribution, amounts of materials, processing, take-back, and reprocessing required for the product of service (geography, geology, chemistry, material science, and engineering)
- The effects of the required product-of-service operation on all life (biology, environmental science)
- The effects of removing products-of-ownership materials from the waste stream (medical science, environmental science)
- The marketing implications of such a changeover (marketing, psychology)
- Full-cost pricing and TTL accounting (economics, sustainable business)
- The history of both ownership and leasing (history)
- The psychology of both ownership and leasing (psychology, marketing)

Although executives in larger companies often have the ability to assign in-house specialists in the aforementioned disciplines to research these questions, rarely is this information synthesized into a single, integrated assessment document, which would greatly assist effective decision-making. A formal education experience that teaches the principles of sustainable business and cultivates this comprehensive, integrative skill set will produce movement leaders and change agents that have the competency to design and interpret these types of assessments.

5.2 Field-Based Education

As previously discussed, a factor that has contributed to the intensifying legacy of environmental damage and natural-resource exploitation has been our failure to recognize the irreplaceable and vital contributions of the natural world to humankind. So many levels of industrial process lie between developed-world humans and the land that the average citizen makes little or no conscious connection between his physical needs and the natural-world sources. We may not even consider that the meal we enjoy in our favorite restaurant actually originates anywhere else but inside our familiar urban landscape. If asked, most of us would respond that the oxygen we breathe is limitless, and the climate all life enjoys is an immutable fixture of the world. Younger generations particularly feel very little connection with Mother Earth and definitely do not see a need to act in her best interest.

A few others that came before us felt otherwise. Nineteenth century philosopher and author Henry David Thoreau believed that we need the unfettered natural world to continually restore our human spirit. John Muir, the turn-of-the-century Scottish naturalist and author, was convinced that all humans need the wilderness to connect with their God. Aldo Leopold wrote that the survival of humankind depends upon natural places to appreciate and study as an example of healthy and durable communities.[13] If the natural world is the irreplaceable source for all our material needs, then our education mandate includes instruction for universally positive endeavors based on an *intimate familiarity* with our life-giving natural community. This reunion between people and the land will foster an appreciation for nature's innumerable contributions to the human experience. Since we tend to care only for things we value, this reconnection brings about a new concern for our expanded concept of community and a commitment to positively contribute to the natural world.

Field-based instruction offers educators an opportunity to convey an *intimate familiarity* with the natural world to an audience. Regardless of the age of the student, the experience of seeing and examining natural processes and concepts first-hand, in real time, heightens the consciousness and enhances the learning process of the student.[14] Environmental concepts that are difficult to explain within the traditional classroom setting are often illustrated very effectively

---

[13] See Leopold (1938) for a persuasive and insightful essay titled "The River of the Mother of God" that suggests various types of value that the wilderness provides.

[14] See Foskett (1997) for more about the advantages of field-based natural-world instruction.

in the outdoors. Outdoor experiential education does require both planning and spontaneity, but the payoffs are often clear applications of specific conceptual messages and long-term retention of the lessons learned.[15]

Let us now briefly consider how a college professor might incorporate valuable field-based experiences into an introductory environmental studies course. After discussing in the classroom the energy and materials strategy for the natural world, a trip to a natural setting to review these concepts while pointing out specific natural-world examples will make a lasting and clear impression in the minds of most students. After lecturing indoors about soil erosion, leading the students outside and showing them specific examples of erosion and the human activities that caused each instance will be worth the time and effort. To facilitate understanding about the role of detritus organisms, consider having a group of students lie down on a forest floor, remove the leaf litter, push aside the partially decaying debris, actually smell the odor of decomposition, and look for the diminutive fauna at work. As convenient and time-efficient as indoor projector slides and images may seem, a direct outdoor experience of an environmental concept using a variety of human senses draws many students into a more meaningful and lasting appreciation of the subject at hand. Also, unplanned opportunities for additional learning and for experiencing outdoor processes will nearly always present themselves to the observant and patient instructor.

In addition to kindling an active, functioning relationship with the natural world through direct encounters, field experiences that inform the life-long learner about social and business conditions within his or her community are also critical for building a solid foundation for effective sustainable business development. In order to arrange TTL social contributions, business participants build a solid grounding in their municipal landscape with first-hand encounters and cultivated relationships at all community levels and service association types. Formal education has the opportunity to systematize social interpretation and relationship-building field trips in a variety of

---

[15] See Lisowski and Disinger (1991).

urban settings, such as distinct neighborhoods, ethnic communities, non-profit offices, and governmental facilities, so as to encounter community advocates and leaders who are the experts at identifying the critical needs of the community. This approach to expanding community relationships is actually *biomimetic* in nature as we emulate the myriad of functioning inter-relationships in the ecosystems of the world by strengthening our spirit of kinship, equality, and unity of purpose within our municipalities.

Arranging an urban field experience for a sustainability-themed high school- or college-level class will capture the opportunity to more firmly imprint the nuances of the movement to the student. Touring an intelligently designed organization facility that is seriously engaged in sustainable business transition provides an opportunity to see firsthand the positive effects of both preferred building characteristics and the TTL innovations of selected operation processes. This experience will eliminate the gap for students between movement theory and practical application of tour-highlighted principles and will provide an opportunity for featured organizations to cooperate with education professionals in providing meaningful social contributions and value.

An interdisciplinary approach to education, the inter-relationship between the natural world and humankind, and the practice of field-based education in both environmental and built landscape requires substantial time, effort, and expense for administrators, teachers, and support staff. Since our intention is to produce citizens who will bring about lasting progress through broadened perspectives and the ability to intelligently solve deep problems, this sizeable investment is necessary and prudent. This major adjustment in education focus will equip generations with the ability to continually refine movement principles and practices and to build healthy, prosperous, and durable communities.

5.3 Re-Educate the Educators

Educators are often some of the brightest and best-informed minds within their field of expertise. They spend their professional careers identifying key information for their students and developing the ability of their class members to critically process challenging concepts. Many instructors in higher education have practitioner experience inside their disciplines and challenge their audience with exercises that require the application of theory to real-life situations. Educators typically go about their business as dedicated, underpaid, and sometimes unappreciated members of the workforce. They hold very dear the freedom to determine the content and pedagogical approach in their classroom and generally resist attempts by anyone or any program to influence their instruction content or approach. So with this picture in mind in Chapter 5, we will discuss amending and enhancing some key parts of the formal curriculum of our educators with sustainability principles while respecting the broader issue of academic freedom.

A common administrative expectation for educators at all levels is to continue professional development within the discipline and to incorporate appropriate content addenda into their instructional materials. Established methods for keeping up-to-date with discipline-wide advancements include professional publications, conferences, and on- and off-site training sessions. Each of these mechanisms could be used to advance foundational sustainability principles and discipline-specific applications of these principles at all levels of formal education. For example, self-starting, self-taught educators who have acquired the relevance of sustainability inside their discipline have the opportunity to author instructional articles for various publications and give corresponding presentations at professional forums. College and university faculty could choose research topics dealing with sustainability issues inside their fields of study and report the findings to colleagues via professional journals and conferences. Education administrators have the opportunity to hire competent sustainability education consultants to organize a series of presentations for their faculty.

Schools, colleges, and universities that take this progressive approach to education reform demonstrate courageous leadership and the critical collaboration necessary to significantly advance the movement even further and faster into mainstream culture. Other efforts to support the diffusion of the suggested education amendments could also include the addition of this type of professional development activity in the tenure and promotion requirements of educators. This administrative policy change would convey the message that the institution recognizes the significance of the movement and that it intends to embrace the evolution of formal education within a sustainability context.

5.4 Obstacles for Education Reform

The positive changes suggested in the previous sections present significant challenges for reform proponents. Let us now discuss the obstacles that complicate the task of large-scale education revision for change agents. The first impediment is the established approach of scholars and higher education to engage the physical sciences, biological sciences, and social sciences separately and to encourage independent specialized study within each discipline. We have artificially seggregated biology from chemistry from physics and de-emphasized the reality of interconnectedness of all science in order to simply our study of the natural world. Even the social sciences of history, economics, and political science have application and connections with natural science and the physical world. Let us take a look at some of man's early decisions that form the basis for our inclination to segregate the various classical disciplines of study and to pursue an individual area of knowledge.

The tendency to specialize roles in our general provisioning task began thousands of years ago when man incorporated agriculture or intensive fishing into his opportunistic scavenging lifestyle. When a successful farming or fishing operation consistently provided an excess of food for a group, individuals within the community developed tool-making skills, social organizational talents, construction aptitude, and religious prowess that were traded for a portion of the food surplus. As society matured and different types of formal inquiry intensified and diversified, the empirical sciences and humanities independently developed. Gainful professional occupations and the accompanying requisite extensive training have continued throughout history to narrow in focus.

Today, in the industrialized world, we find a preponderance of respected specialists that know their single professional field but that do not have a clear understanding about how their specialty relates to other fields of endeavor. This inability to perceive and function within existing interdisciplinary relationships has handicapped our understanding of natural laws and trends within our world. When individual members of society act without regard for the interdependence of all our endeavors, unintended insidious negative effects are common. As previously discussed, a substantial portion of the environmental and social perturbations were originally a result of ignorance and have been allowed to continue through many decades to the present.

Our repeated tendency has been to remedy our problems in isolation. An example of such an approach previously discussed is environmentalism, which was intended to solve our pollution and resource exploitation problems but ignored the concerns of business and, to a lesser extent, other related concerns of society. The high costs and relatively disappointing results of this simplistic strategy were considered in Chapter 1. We now recognize this new challenge to adjust our premise for technology and societal progress to include a consideration of all of the effects of a proposed solution in relation to all members of the community.

Humankind indeed has the opportunity to acknowledge our mistakes and to amend our education efforts so that each generation of students understands and appreciates the contributions of various disciplines as well as the interconnections among all fields of study. The visionary R. Buckminster Fuller popularized the term *comprehensivist* to describe someone who moves through life with a keen perspective of the existing relationships among all the arts and sciences.[16] However, when scholars and educators do seriously undertake the ambitious challenge of integrating all disciplines, the positive results will manifest gradually as new classes of graduates are exposed to increasing emphasis on comprehensivist thinking.

And so another obstacle for the movement appears: until our education systems implement the full set of meaningful changes

---

[16] See Fuller (1969) for an insightful expose on the trend of specialized learning in higher education.

suggested in this chapter, most existing business leaders will be handicapped when attempting to fully embrace the principles and practices that are germane to the movement. Although the potential to reduce energy costs and increase positive publicity often initially piques the curiosity of business leaders and draws them into sustainable business, robust engagement of the movement is unlikely without an appreciation of the full depth and breadth of the movement. Some larger, for-profit companies have the resources to employ private sustainable business consulting firms for staff education but other smaller-budget organizations do not. So, in addition to amending our traditional education system, another major challenge exists to provide an opportunity for current professionals to understand Earth's compromised situation and the principles of the movement that offer a viable long-term solution to our dilemma.

Bringing inquiring professionals "up to speed" with the movement might appear much easier than affecting change throughout formal education, but closer consideration and experience reveals sizeable obstacles on this front as well. Seasoned business people often have the most difficulty embracing sustainable business. This broad group, although sometimes curious, are generally skeptical and somewhat closed-minded about the paradigm-busting concepts of the movement. Executives and most managers at large organizations, accustomed to receiving new bodies of information in clearly written report summaries, may expect the entire essence of the movement to be contained in an after-lunch presentation. The reason for this attitude is probably that today's working professionals were educated under our prevailing educational system and most likely have limited familiarity with natural-world systems or social situations outside their own socioeconomic level. They are often at a stage of life where a serious paradigm challenge may prove too unsettling and would require too much emotional energy. These folks are looking to streamline their business and personal affairs, not turn the apple cart upside down. Actually considering *a complete remake of how business is done* can overwhelm the normally unflappable executive.

When an experienced executive or manager buys into the movement, he or she inevitably accepts both *personal and professional complicity* in the root problems of business that make the revolution necessary in the first place. Ownership of that revelation is often a difficult struggle for some people. The counter notion — other people were and are the ones responsible for the problems — is much more palatable. So movement educators that engage established business professionals will do well to remember that some in their audience cannot, or will not, accept the emotional earthquake required of the conversion. When some people first come to understand the nature, scope, and source of the environmental and social problems, they react with disbelief, fear, and even denial. Often the best choice for the educator in that case is to concentrate on the more receptive members of the audience. At the same time, the experienced professional often richens the sustainable business education discussion with discriminating questions and different perspectives that benefit the facilitator and audience as well.

5.5 The Operations Side of Education

Another challenge for higher education administrators who commit to the movement is the remodeling of day-to-day operations of the learning institutions themselves so as to reflect sustainability values. Even for the newly involved institution, searching the workplace for opportunities to make TTL advancements can yield a surprising number of opportunities. When administrators tackle the challenge with a team of eager revisionists, even more "low-hanging fruit" appears. Energy options, building renovation and design, furniture and work station considerations, indoor air quality, day-to-day material purchases, landscaping choices, food-service composting, employee compensation packages, and partnerships within the local community are just a few examples of operational TTL enhancement opportunities for each committed campus community.

Colleges and universities find that implementing operational reform is most challenging at the beginning of the process, when effective training, staff buy-in, and TTL process establishment are critical. As the reform effort progresses, a positive, stimulating, and unity-building professional atmosphere often takes shape. Each thoughtfully conceived and implemented movement innovation increases the economic, environmental, and social performance of the institution as well as builds its public recognition as an ambitious leader in academia. As sustainability literacy increases throughout society's mainstream, the growing number of TTL operational improvements, along with the noteworthy curricular changes, will increasingly define the positive reputation of the learning institution. These early explicit advantages provide a springboard for the forward-thinking institution in the competitive world of higher education not only for private schools but also for public institutions. At the same time, each cutting-edge college, university, or even school district will be moving our species one step closer to an abundant, beautiful, and healthy legacy to pass on to future generations.

5.6 An Academic Prototype

The best reform intentions can be hamstrung in the absence of a practical and effective process that encourages innovation. Up to this point in the movement, no single process design has fit the needs of all types and sizes of educational institutions. As nature reminds us, although the same set of universal natural laws applies to each member of each community, using diverse approaches to follow these guidelines is the rule in the natural world. Although the recipe for sustainable operations is somewhat specific for each organization, the following example of a college with an unusual and effective TTL design process for operations is presented for the purpose of stimulating productive thought and dialogue.

In the spring semester of 2006, Aquinas College, a small-liberal arts school in Grand Rapids, MI, began the implementation of a new program called the Aquinas Sustainability Initiative. The story begins in the previous summer when the provost called for a strategy that would act as a framework to transform Aquinas to a "sustainable campus." A basic plan was crafted by a faculty member in late September and, after inviting a number of interested faculty and staff to the refining process, the idea was deemed ready for the challenging implementation procedure. School officials searched but could not find any other college or university that had attempted similar sustainable-operation improvements, so no frame of reference was available. Nevertheless, the administration was onboard with the plan, a number of key faculty and staff took ownership, and the sustainability ball was rolling; but unfortunately, considerable obstacles lay ahead.

The traditional method for significant operational change in similar institutions is for the design, scope, and marching orders of a particular project to come from the top of the organization. Examples that might reflect current sustainability literacy include a LEED-certified building project, a materials cycling program, or a decision to permanently adjust the campus thermostats. Funding must be secured, top administration approval garnered, the board of trustees consulted, and then a college presidential proclamation declared that the new program is operational. But such was not the case for this bold initiative. This plan was unproven, unconventional, and organically rooted within the *entire* campus community. The intention was not to capture headlines but rather to put into place a plan where every operational aspect of the college was reviewable and available for change by all members of the campus community. Even if Aquinas officials had opted to make a press release of the endeavor, few in the region would have understood or taken much notice.

Interestingly, the original architect of the initiative chose the lack of understanding of value-producing sustainability principles by the campus community as the most important situation in need of remedy, and as such, member engagement and education was paramount. Leaders of the faculty, staff, and student assemblies were first called together for a series of informational meetings to explain the components of the initiative. The eventual goals of the plan were to have TTL-operational changes continually submitted by faculty, staff, and students, the initiatives refined by a campus committee with an expertise in sustainable principles, and the finished initiatives then sent for a vote to the respective assembly of the original submitter, and if passed, given to the provost for approval and implementation. Fortunately, each assembly leader supported the overall plan and presented information and a motion to form a new-standing sustainability committee within their membership. All three of the campus governing bodies were required to approve the proposal in its entirety or the Aquinas College Sustainability Initiative would have been scrapped.

At that point in time, many faculty, staff, and students were somewhat familiar with the sustainable business movement. In 2003, the College had established the first Sustainable Business Bachelor of Science degree program in the nation, and by then this signature program had generated numerous conversations across the campus. Strategically, the student assembly first took on the sustainability initiative measure and passed the legislation with very few members voting against it. Next, the staff assembly, with the help of a handful of key leaders, also passed the measure with a bit more skeptical dissent than was generated in the student assembly discussion. Finally, a lengthy and spirited discussion in the faculty assembly ended with the narrowest margin of victory for the initiative. The measure, which included permanent-standing sustainability committees, had passed all three required assemblies and became formally institutionalized across the College in April 2006. But the work had just begun.

Fortunately by this time, the *Center for Sustainability at Aquinas College* was established with permanent staff, student workers, and a comprehensive, functioning Website. The Center staff agreed to receive the initial on-line initiative idea submissions from faculty, staff, and students of the College. From that point, each initiative submission was assigned to a refinement team of senior-level sustainable business students. The Center staff also agreed to record the progress of each submission through the entire process on the initiative webpage. After the initiative was submitted and refined, it was sent to the corresponding assembly sustainability committee to undergo a rating process. Each committee then rated ideas from their constituents in terms of potential to produce TTL value for the school on a 1–5 scale, with 4 and 5 representing positive recommendations for passage. After obtaining the TTL rating, the initiative moved to the full assembly for an approve/not approve vote. All assembly-approved submissions were sent to the provost office for implementation. Any initiatives voted down were returned to the submitter, who was invited to a restructuring process hosted by senior sustainable business students.

At the same time the sustainability initiative process began to take shape, a variety of sustainability education events were planned for the campus community. Sustainability guest speakers were brought to campus, with the general public also invited to attend these lectures. The Sustainable Business Department faculty made open presentations on various sustainability topics, and teams of sustainable business students visited classrooms around the entire campus when invited and shared their knowledge with non-majors and various instructors. A small group of faculty expressed a particular interest to learn more about the movement and how they might incorporate sustainability principles into their own courses. Lunchtime meetings were organized with interested faculty to facilitate discussion about improving overall understanding of the movement and embedding sustainability principles into the general curriculum.

It is duly noted that the opportunity for students, staff, and faculty to engage in a process for positive change in campus operations did not resonate with all community members. Even though a grant provided funds to finance the innovations, a large sector of campus stakeholders remained ambivalent or skeptical. Some chose not to take advantage of the educational opportunities, and others cited schedule conflicts with the programs. Initiative organizers learned that changing a fundamental part of the college's culture is indeed challenging and time-consuming. Simply managing the initiative proposal process required many staff hours per month, and collaborating with other community members for process improvements devoured even more time and effort.

Also duly noted, in addition to the many operational improvements that came from the sustainability initiative, a variety of unplanned subtle benefits also surfaced around the campus. Students, staff, and faculty found themselves working together for a number of tangible goals outside of the formal education process. Solid relationships formed among people who hardly knew one another before the initiative had brought them together. A sense of unity of purpose had begun to break down professional walls and social distinction. The president of the College attended classroom presentations on pending student initiatives. A janitor, department head, and a pair of students were seen in the hallway discussing an initiative proposal. Alumni and parents of students, all intrigued by the initiative, began inquiring if they could submit innovation ideas. Today, sustainability committee positions are now some of the most sought-after assembly assignments, with music professors, maintenance personnel, accountants, and geography students as examples of those filling the slots.

The following is a sample of approved and implemented initiative changes:

- A campus policy that gives preference to student art for decorating the interior of campus buildings
- An Aquinas Website that posts car-pooling opportunities among the commuting student population
- Installation of 20 locally manufactured bike racks around various campus locations
- A free campus bike-use program for the entire campus community
- Regular electronics cycling opportunities for the entire campus community
- A campus office paper purchase policy for only 100% post-consumer, chlorine-free cycled content, with Forest Stewardship Council Certification and Green Seal Certification

Rather than adapting a program where only high-ranking administrators make the decisions concerning the appropriate features for a sustainable campus, Aquinas College chose a different method. Taking its lead from the natural world that provides all types of creatures an opportunity to contribute to the richness of the community, the sustainability initiative offers a direct role to all campus members in using the TTL as the standard for innovation. The intent is to facilitate change guided by economic stability, natural-world support, and a positive connection with the neighbors; the outcome has been a payment of sustainable dividends, one idea at a time.

5.7 Research and the Movement

Another opportunity for academia in the sustainable transition business involves full-time faculty who work at colleges and universities throughout the world. Most higher education academics have research responsibilities; some devote a large part of their professional time conducting and publishing research, while others concentrate on teaching assignments and assume only a modicum of research activity. Today, faculty members who find themselves on any part of this continuum have a chance to engage in research that supports the emerging field of sustainable business and their own particular discipline. Many favorable opportunities exist today for both quantitative and qualitative projects in fields such as biology, chemistry, economics, energy, environmental science, geography, material science, political science, sociology, public policy, and urban planning. With the recent genesis of sustainable business, the original nature of the movement provides wide-open questions and topics for applied inquiry. Investigating the multitude of relationships among natural-world systems and human processes has only begun to be addressed by the scientific community. College and university administrators can incentivize this new approach by setting research and tenure policies that credit movement-related research activities equal to, or above, the traditionally specialized fields of study.

A number of challenges do exist today for the professor who is interested in investigating sustainability topics. Active researchers will have a relatively small body of established knowledge to build upon but at the same time will find a wide variety of unanswered questions for investigation. A relatively small number of established professional journals exist that publish sustainable practices research, so garnering an appropriate level of peer exposure and review for the work may initially prove a challenge. Arranging a suitable source of funding to support this non-conventional research bent may require research professionals to cultivate some new creative underwriting sources. A final consideration is the extent of the researcher's multidisciplinary background and the potentially steep learning curve for sustainability research topics, when compared to single discipline concentrations. While this short list of formal research impediments may sound quite daunting, crafting solutions that deliver a solid foundation for sustainability investigation is certainly within the capacity for new and seasoned investigators alike. An increasing number of successful projects will continue to add to our meaningful body of knowledge, increase movement credibility within the empirical science community, and provide supporting evidence to answer some of the critical issues that remain on the sustainable business agenda.

5.8 The Interdisciplinary Aspect

A survey of the current academic landscape in the U.S. yields only a handful of sustainable business programs that grant a degree. As intimated in the first part of this chapter, a number of obstacles exist for infusing meaningful sustainability concepts into established disciplines at all levels of education. Although sustainable business is evolving and developing, the movement has not yet had the time to fully mature into an accepted discipline; indeed, more study, academic review, and professional journals devoted to this field are needed to complete the transition. This type of extended maturation process has been common for many established disciplines and is part of the natural course of events for sustainable business as well.

During this period of flux and development, several pioneer programs have emerged in higher education to take the lead in this ambitious enterprise. In the face of varying degrees of academic skepticism, a number of creditable college-level sustainable business programs offer a viable option for anyone seriously interested in acquiring a meaningful understanding of the evolving principles of the movement. Both undergraduate and graduate programs have formed and are beginning to meet the growing demand for a dependable source of qualified graduates who are prepared to guide the triple top-line aspirations in a variety of organizational settings. As valuable as this unique proficiency is for employees today, the benefits will only increase as the professional moves through his or her career.

As sustainable business practices further permeate mainstream commerce, the entire formal education system is challenged to further adapt and develop a reliable source to produce an up-to-date applied comprehensivist graduate.

However, obstacles do exist for the establishment of multidisciplinary sustainable business programs and departments at the college level, particularly for the larger universities. We have discussed the limited theoretic and applied sustainable business expertise among college faculty in general as a barrier to expansion. Another formidable impediment in the formation of these programs is simply getting commitments from chairpersons and faculty of various departments to work together on an interdisciplinary program. Competition for institutional resources among established departments is often keen at colleges and universities, so propositions that involve changes in faculty responsibilities with little direct and measurable departmental benefit can be a difficult sell. Because departments often view each other as competing entities, "turf-guarding" among disciplines is quite common in academia. Administrators can influence decisions concerning department collaboration with interdisciplinary programs by offering tangible support for such participation, such as additional faculty positions, tenure and promotion currency, and opportunity for professional education in sustainable business.

5.9 The Academic Program and Curricula

The design of college-level sustainable business programs thus far has taken a variety of approaches. A commonality among current efforts is the multidisciplinary curricula, which often includes biology, chemistry, physics, various social sciences, environmental science, conventional business, and sustainable business. Both undergraduate- and graduate-level plans of study are offered by a few resolute colleges and universities. The following sections summarize some notable college and university programs in the U.S. to date.

5.10 Current Undergraduate Programs

Aquinas College, Grand Rapids, MI

Degree Title – Bachelor of Science in Sustainable Business
Year Founded – 2003
Number of Graduates (as of 2009): 41

Required Courses

Financial Accounting	Managerial Accounting
Principles of Management	Principles of Marketing
Financial Management	Business Ethics
Introduction to Communication	Microeconomics
Environmental Biology	Environmental Chemistry
Physical Science	Intro to Environmental Studies
Advanced Environmental Studies	Building Social Capital
Cases in Sustainable Business	Industrial Ecology
Sustainable Business Management	Sustainable Business
Innovations Lab	Internship

Plus Two of the Following Three Courses:

Environmental Regulatory Compliance
Environmental Economics and Policy
Sustainable Energy Systems

Arizona State University, Tempe, AZ

Degree Title – Bachelor of Arts in Business with a Concentration in
Sustainability
Year Founded – 2008
Number of Graduates (as of 2009) – 0

Required Courses

Accounting I	Accounting II
Computer Information Technology	Business Statistics

Principles of Marketing
Fundamentals of Finance
International Business
Microeconomics
English Composition
Sustainable Cities
Calculus II

Management & Leadership
Global Supply Operations
Ethical & Regulatory Issues
Macroeconomics
A Sustainable World
Calculus I

Plus Four of the Following Seven Courses:

Society and Sustainability
International Sustainability
Sustainable Energy & Materials
Policy, Planning, and Governance

Economics of Sustainability
Sustainable Urban Dynamics
Sustainable Ecosystems

Catawba College, Salisbury, NC

Degree Title – Bachelor of Science in Sustainable Business &
    Community Development
Year Founded – 2007
Number of Graduates (as of 2009) – 0

Required Courses

Principles of Accounting
Business Law
Business Ethics
Principles of Marketing
Principles of Economics
Bioscience

Managerial Finance
Principles of Management
Management of Small Business
Public Relations
Environmental Economics
Chemistry and the
    Environment

Environmental Science
Management
Ecological Change and Human
    Health
Capstone in Environmental Studies

Resource Ecology and
    Sustainable Community Plan
Sustainable Facilities Internship

5.11 Graduate Programs

Bainbridge Graduate Institute, Bainbridge Island, WA

Degree Title – MBA in Sustainable Business
Year Founded – 2002

Number of Graduates (as of 2008) – 150

Required Courses
Finance, Accounting & The Triple Bottom-Line
Marketing & Sales
Management I: People and Teams
Management II: Organizational Systems
Management III: Organizational Change
Entrepreneurship & Intrapreneurship
Neoclassical & Ecological Economics
Capitalism & Political Economics
Leadership and Personal Development
Strategy and Implementation
Quantitative Research Methods
Systems Thinking in Action
Responsible Capitalism
Social Justice and Business
Creativity & Right Livelihood
Foundations in Sustainable Business
Sustainable Operations

Duquesne University, Pittsburgh, PA

Degree Title – MBA Sustainability
Year Founded – 2007
Number of Graduates (as of 2008) – 0

Required Courses

Financial & Managerial Accounting	Advanced Accounting
Financial Management	Advanced Marketing

Public Affairs Management   Organizational Behavior
Applied Ethics   Applied Economics & Statistics
Value Chain & Operations   Systems Thinking
   Strategy
Environmental Science   Strategy Capstone
Sustainability Theories and Models Sustainability Applications
Change in Sustainable Enterprises Sustainability Project

Presidio World College, San Francisco, CA

Degree Title – MBA in Sustainable Management
Year Founded – 2003
Number of Graduates (as of 2008) – 56

Required Courses

Effective Management &   Managerial Marketing
   Communication
Business, Government &   Managerial Finance
   Civil Society
Managerial Economics   Ecological Economics
Managerial Accounting   Integrative Capstone
Strategic Management   Venture Plan
Operations and Production
Culture, Value & Ethics
Economics, Capital Markets & The Law
Leadership for Sustainable Management
Sustainable Products and Services
Sustainable Business Practice Implementation
Principles of Sustainable Management

Arizona State University, Tempe, AZ

Degree Title: Ph.D. in Sustainability
Year Founded – 2007
Number of Graduates (as of 2008) – 0

Required Courses
Urban Growth

Water Quality & Scarcity	State Land Workshop
Water Policy & Management	Sustainable Ecosystems
Institutions, Environment,	Intellectual Issues
and Society	Urban Growth
Climate Change Adaptation	Social Transformations
Workshop	

Advanced Earth Systems Engineering
Science, Technology, and Public Affairs
Urban Ecological Systems
Principles of Sustainability
Quantitative Methods in Sustainability
Science for Sustainability
Sustainable Energy and Material Use
Human Dimensions of Sustainability
Industrial Ecology and Design
International Development & Sustainability
Statistics for Sustainability
Introduction to Sustainability in Organizations
Sustainable Transportation Systems

This chapter outlines specific improvements for formal education that will continue to move valuable sustainability principles into academia. The importance of recognizing interdisciplinary connections and embedding experiential field-based pedagogy in all levels of formal education is explained. The ongoing need to re-educate our educators and to overcome the obstacles that stand in the way of meaningful reform is also proffered. We discuss the logical revamping of the operational policies of our learning institutions to reflect the growing commitment of the education community for sustainable living systems. Finally, examples of existing college-level degree-granting sustainable business programs are summarized.

These multifaceted education reforms empower our schools to reflect an operational and philosophical commitment to the movement. In the next chapter, we consider the appropriate role of government in this ongoing revolution. Like nearly all intelligent changes of the movement, we will discover how government reform measures can be structured to solve a number of serious social problems simultaneously. We discuss the opportunity to simplify and redirect public and environmental policy to encourage the long-term health and fecundity of our local communities and the world at large. We consider government economic policies that reward sustainable industrial design and that penalize operations that degrade the community. We bring together policy-makers, conventional business leaders, sustainable business experts, social advocates, and ecologists in order to put into place appropriate economic incentives and disincentives that will encourage durable, healthy, and beautiful regions across our landscape.

Guide Point 5: A formal education system that incorporates sustainability principles at all levels will provide an important component of the social infrastructure that is required to deeply embed sustainable business into our modern culture.

Chapter 6

Government Finally Gets It Right

The following is the Preamble of the Constitution for the United States of America that was signed into law on 17 September 1787:

> We the People of the United States, in Order to form a more perfect Union, establish Justice, insure domestic Tranquility, provide for the common defense, promote the general Welfare, and secure the Blessings of Liberty to ourselves and our Posterity, do ordain and establish this Constitution for the United States of America.

Two clear messages contained in this passage have direct relevance to the sustainable business movement. The Preamble expresses an intention of the constitution to provide a framework that would first "promote the general Welfare" and second, "secure the Blessings of Liberty to ourselves and our Posterity." Both of these intentions underpin a quite similar ambition of the sustainable business movement — to promote and secure the welfare of the current generation and of future generations. Today, more than 200 years removed from the signing of the U.S. Constitution, sustainable business pioneers have aligned with our founding fathers in this far-reaching commitment. The difference in approaches to achieving this goal notwithstanding, we do stand united across time in our purpose and intent.

In this chapter we will consider the nature and scope of appropriate government involvement in the ongoing evolution of sustainable business. In the first section, the proper role of government as a subordinate movement supporter rather than an architect of movement principles will be examined. Next, strategies for crafting effective TTL policies and relevant corporate reform measures will be outlined. The last part of the chapter will discuss operational changes for government itself that will deliver increased day-to-day value to the taxpayers and will provide a procedural foundation for effective management of public revenue and of bureaucratic staff. We will primarily focus upon the situation and role of the federal government, but state and local jurisdictions will be examined as well.

6.1 Not Repeating Mistakes

We will begin with a discussion of the issue of government regulation and sustainable business. As visionaries Leopold and McDonough both adroitly posited more than 50 years apart, government is unable to lead a consequential social movement that provides an opportunity for durable prosperity for all. Leopold, in his 1938 lecture to the University of Wisconsin, College of Engineering (titled *Engineering and Conservation*), emphasized that any meaningful change involving industry, the natural world, and society would be led by private citizens.[17] McDonough and co-author Michael Braungart assert in their 2002 book *Cradle to Cradle* that government regulation is a signal of design failure and that a much more intelligent goal is industrial processes that need no regulation. These two statements capture two themes of sustainable business: ownership of the movement by private individuals and the re-design of industry for TTL value production.

As explained previously, the U.S. environmental regulatory policy of the last 50 years has shown to be very expensive and largely ineffective. Continuing this strategy is analogous to sopping up spilled paint from a hole in the bottom of a paint can before plugging the hole. The government understands little about how to best sop up the paint and even less about the need to immediately plug the hole in the can. Government functions very differently than for-profit businesses and does not have the capacity to "fix" root problems of the private sector. Clearly, allowing government to regulate away the *symptoms* of the deep economic, environmental, and social dilemmas of business is and has always been a losing proposition.

---

[17] See Flader and Callicott (1991) for Aldo Leopold's 1938 incredibly visionary essay on the need for a new approach to business by businesses that respects the land and people.

If we accept the limits of government regulation in this regard, how then will we instruct government to effectively support the movement? Paul Hawken, Avery Lovins, and L. Hunter Lovins smartly advocate a restructuring of our federal system of economic incentives and disincentives. In the book *Natural Capitalism*, they point out how the federal government's greatest instrument for influencing the activities of citizens is the tax system. The authors explain how the federal tax system bases the amount of tax it levies on profit and labor and, thereby, discourages profits and artificially raises the cost of each employee for business. Government is using a seriously flawed strategy for raising operation funds that discourages two things, profits and jobs, which are both vital for vibrant communities. Instead of discouraging positive community contributions, government could base its tax levy on things detrimental to society such as pollution, greenhouse gas emissions, resource exploitation, and international capital investments.

Hawken and Lovins also make suggestions for reforming current government economic incentive programs that encourage activities that are detrimental to citizens. They cite policies based on antiquated mining laws that continually sell mineral rights on federal land for pennies on the dollar of its market value or national forest timber harvest agreements that undervalue the timber and finance the roads required to harvest the trees for the timber company. Subsidizing tobacco farmers to grow a set amount of their crop, which contributes to nearly half a million smoking-related deaths in the U.S. each year, is another example of an unwise federal government economic incentive program. Reforming economic incentive policies to encourage only positive contributions to society, such as more organically grown food, sustainable energy, and locally owned healthy businesses, makes much more sense. Certainly, the specific stipulations and terms of these suggested incentive programs are critical for success, but a significant opportunity exists for government to restructure its incentive and disincentive programs in ways that effectively restrain activities not in the best interest of community members and that support sustainable business practices and principles. In the next section, we will examine the process involved in organizing effective policy that generates these types of desirable results.

6.2 Crafting Sustainable Business Policy

With leaders of formal education systems recognizing the value of embedding sustainable principles into their curricula and operations, the general public's connection to the movement will proliferate and grow. The sophistication level of the news media will correspondingly increase, which will improve the quality of information available to the public about the movement. The desire of the voters will intensify for economic policy incentives and disincentives to reflect the expanding sustainability ethic. Politicians at various levels will then assume the arduous task of organizing an overhaul of government policies that reward organizations for TTL value production and penalize businesses that lack this multifaceted utility.

At this point it is useful to note a reality in U.S. politics that further challenges political support for the movement and effective policy creation. The length of term for federal and state political office holders typically varies from two years (U.S. Congress) to six years (U.S. Senate). Often, the traceable benefits from sustainable business policy do not surface for multiple years and, as such, the recognition for politicians who support these measures is delayed, sometimes past their term in office. With so many career politicians these days, splashy problem-of-the-month projects that generally provide immediate political currency often trump long-term commitments. Even though the appreciating benefits from sustainable business policies are enormous, politicians are wont to spend time and resources on issues that will provide leverage for their next re-election campaign. Only a principled public servant that understands the benefits of the movement will likely act in the best interest of his or her constituency and actively support sustainable business policies.

Historically, political policy-making in the U.S. has been a tumultuous and contentious process. Politicians on all sides of an issue typically wrangle and joist in power plays that most often support the agenda of a particularly well-connected special interest group or groups rather than the best interests of the politicians' full constituencies. Surprisingly to those not involved in policy formation, the best interest of all citizens involved in a particular policy rarely even enters into private discussion. Politicians and bureaucrats stubbornly push the narrow interests of their closest supporters or their supervisors' supporters. These lengthy policy negotiations generally end in favoring the more powerful politicians' agenda with compromises in accord with the political ammunition of the other side. The actual terms and substance of the policy are spun by each political camp in ways that benefit their interests and discredit rival opposition leaders.

An unusual circumstance that does change these policy-making dynamics is a *political mandate*, which involves an overwhelmingly one-sided public opinion on a particular issue. On rare occasions, public sentiment concerning an issue is exceedingly strong and only minor opposition exists, such as with President Franklin Roosevelt's New Deal legislation, the repeal of prohibition by the 21st Amendment, the U.S. entering into World War II after the Japanese attack on Pearl Harbor, and the 2003 invasion of Iraq after the terrorist attack of the U.S. on 11 September, 2001. Other less recognizable political mandates have arisen and have resulted in a relatively speedy and civil process of policy-creation.

On the sustainable business front, the broad-based nature and momentum of the movement will continue to attract a wide variety of supporters, including business owners and employees, economic development organizers, environmental champions, and social advocates. With schools districts, colleges and universities, the news media, and private businesses all fulfilling their educational role, the groundswell of sustainable sentiment will provide a solid foundation for the establishment of decisive TTL policy at a variety of governmental levels. Federal, state, county, and municipal legislators have the fortuitous opportunity to follow a visionary course and construct coordinated systems of policy incentives and disincentives for the strategic benefit of generations to come.

[The specific method with which policyorganizers proceed will largely affect the success of these efforts. Fortunately, movement frontrunners and savvy organization leaders have learned a beneficial lesson in terms of team-based process innovation, which can be transferred to the policy-making process. The makeup and backgrounds of the individuals in the policy-making group is critical. A skilled and unbiased process leader, a movement expert, an experienced policy bureaucrat, a representative for business, and at least two general citizens from different socioeconomic backgrounds are all essential members. Other stakeholders such as an ecologist or social scientist can fill out the committee representation, along with any others uniquely affected by the particular policy.

After assembling an appropriately diverse team, the next step is for the leader to begin policy formation discussion with TTL production as the overriding goal. The process leader solicits input from each member of the committee on each policy consideration but no member is allowed to dominate the proceedings to the exclusion of others. Each member contributes his or her own ideas with a particular concern for the stakeholders that he or she represents within the larger intention of TTL value production. The facilitator acts as an objective and impartial moderator, moving the policymaking session along while including all member contributions for consideration by the team. Actively involving all stakeholders in the TTL policy-crafting process increases the chances of policy-formation that satisfies the needs of all parties affected by the measure.

As mentioned earlier, key to the entire policy-formation process is the use of a skilled and impartial process leader with the responsibility of recording the concerns of each stakeholder and distilling down the collection of ideas into a cohesive and functional body of TTL-generating policy. Today, achieving effective policy often involves a series of revisions of draft policy by persistent teams of reformers. Creativity, patience, a collaborative spirit, and dedication to the principles of sustainable business are other characteristics of effective policy architects.

At this point in our discussion of government policy-making, it is interesting to note the difference in emphasis of sustainability policy between the U.S. and Western European nations. Governments in Western Europe have taken more of a passive role in business sector reform compared to the U.S. Meaningful change for European nations nearly always originates from voluntary operational reform inside the private sector, with governmental policy influences proving less consequential. On the other side of the Atlantic, U.S.

industry has a history of environmental and social operational changes instigated only as a result of specific federal government policies. An important attitudinal adjustment incumbent upon U.S. business leaders entering the sustainable business campaign is accepting the responsibility for significant process change inside their own organizations. The notion that the government's role is to set private organizational standards for sustainable business innovation does not best serve the individual business or the movement. Because of fundamental differences between governments and private enterprise, politicians rarely have the ability to independently determine specific and appropriate sustainable business operational change. As U.S. industry recognizes and accepts its role to develop meaningful innovation and to assist in sustainable business policy formation, so will the interests of commerce, government, the natural world, and human society be best served. Next, we will examine the role of government in perhaps the most difficult challenge in the quest to create a durable and healthy commercial system: redefining corporate guidelines.

6.3 Reforming the Corporate Rules

A common and reasonable expectation of government is to maintain a fair set of rules under which business operates. Similarly, a reasonable expectation for business is to provide goods and services while earning a fair profit for its efforts. As discussed previously, an important caveat maintains that "fair profit" is not garnered at the expense of anyone outside of the particular economic transaction (such as an asthmatic missing work on account of high levels of vehicle pollution). Today in the U.S. and around the world, we find different sets of rules and incentives governing locally owned businesses and corporations. Some of these different policy rules are causing (and have been causing for many decades) significant problems for the uniquely valuable locally owned businesses and for society in general. This section considers the relationship between the corporation and sustainable business and will suggest major changes in the laws and regulations that govern corporate activity.

The role of the corporation in the U.S. has changed considerably since the fledgling group of American colonies broke free from oppressive European corporations in the Revolutionary War. Early U.S. corporations were chartered for specific projects like road or bridge building and were dissolved after the venture was completed. Corporation proponents waged a relentless and continual self promotion campaign until the U.S. Supreme Court held in the 1886 case of *Santa Clara County v. Southern Pacific Railroad* that a corporation owns the same rights as a "natural person" with special protections under the law, such as corporate shareholders having only the limited liability of the money they invested for the actions of the corporation. The 14th Amendment to the U.S. Constitution has been used by corporate representatives numerous times since to uphold the "rights" of corporations to continue specific activities that were protested by numerous groups of affected people. With an increasing U.S. population by the end of the 19th century demanding more and more goods and services from a limited production supply, defenders of this unprecedented period of concentrating corporate power cited the need to reduce the investment risk for those considering investing the limited available venture capital into new or expanded production corporations. The corporation, with its special treatment and power, was now the most expedient method of delivering the sorely needed products to the market.

Today, U.S. corporations are run by executives living in completely different locations than most of the physical operations of their companies. Corporate officers are legally bound to make only those decisions that maximize the return on the investment of shareholders, who live in various places around the world. This reality has set the stage for a number of troublesome outcomes for members of the location that is hosting a facility of a corporation. Neither the corporate decision maker nor the investor experiences the effects of operational decisions, such as legally emitting pollution or laying off workers. Nearby community members are forced to absorb externalized adverse side effects with no opportunity for restitution. Corporate farms in the U.S. systematically degrade soil fertility when they choose not to adopt soil-conservation or enrichment practices that would add cost to the current year's crop production but would provide long-term viability of the resource. In developing nations, corporate factory working conditions often lack basic safety features, which results in numerous work-site accidents and chronic exposure to toxic materials. Furthermore, corporations from developed nations routinely exploit natural resources such as forests to the detriment of future generations.

Sustainability author Paul Hawken has long advocated a revision of the government rules under which corporations operate.[18] He reminds us that the special set of conditions granted to corporations was done so to benefit all members of society and advises a revision of the requirements for granting corporate charters by the state so that each corporate facility benefits the locality in which it operates. Taking this idea of corporate reform a step further, we can consider creating a special class of *locally owned and operated corporations* that offers tax-free benefits for all shareholder earnings (similar to current utility stocks). Stock purchase would be available only to local residents, and the companies would be managed by corporate officers required to live in the same locality. With all dividends paid to local shareholders, profits would remain in the local economy to recirculate and enrich the community, and with corporate operations, stockholders, and executives all located within a single community, externalizing costs of production would be much less likely. Astute leaders of these smaller corporations would find partnerships and collaboration opportunities with other small local companies, drawing communities even closer together. As more and more smaller corporations embrace sustainable business, the local makeup of these new companies will naturally be drawn to movement principles, thereby contributing to more stable, productive, and healthy communities.

6.4 Operational Advances for Government

Numerous advantages gained from movement-based operational changes inside for-profit and non-profit organizations are transferable

---

[18] See Hawken's 1993 in a seminal article in which he suggests a number of controversial and insightful changes in business.

to all levels of government bureaucracy. Energy choices, product purchasing, facility design, employee working conditions, and even collaborative ventures with other organizations can be enhanced inside government so as to produce environmental and social value while lowering administrative costs funded by taxpayers. Although politicians normally pay closest attention to key special-interest groups that support their campaigns, issues that generate large volumes of voter comments also get their attention, and as sustainable business doctrine continues to embed in mainstream culture, a demand for similar advances in government operations is inevitable. The rate of TTL change, however, will occur at a considerably slower pace than in private sector organizations because of a number of the following endemic characteristics of government operations that seem counterintuitive for most private business professionals.

First, various taxation and fee programs provide government with its operating revenue. Bureaucratic budgetary decisions are rarely based on the need to cut operating costs and increase surplus; rather bureaucrats quickly learn to spend their entire annual budget or they will likely have their funds cut for the next fiscal year. Second, government employees at all levels are rarely hired solely on their qualifications and expertise but rather because of political favors or associations with politically influential people. Often the education and professional background of a new government employee does not even approach the needs of the position. This sort of bureaucratic incompetence is regularly absorbed into federal, state, and local political systems that do not depend upon excellence for their existence; even public perceptions of politicians who appoint key administrative positions and control the funding levels are only marginally important. Most significant reductions in the scope of government programs are caused by a decrease in the overall tax base available to politicians. Third, the public, even special interest groups, have a difficult time influencing government's own day-to-day operations. The bureaucracy normally has many isolated layers that protect politicians and high-ranking administrators from a discriminating, politically active public sector. Administrative decisions are often self-serving and used to gain political currency for influencing other affairs. For these reasons, sustainable business-based reform, as with all political system reform, will move forward at a considerably slower rate than TTL change from inside the private sector, which constantly looks for competitive advantages. The potential for dramatic operational advancements that would serve the public well is indubitable, but because of the deep systemic problems in government mentioned above, progress in this arena will be slow in coming.

The civic level most receptive to sustainable change is local government, which has leaders who are members of the local community and are generally accessible to constituents. City governments have led the way in implementing positive operational change in support of the movement. Examples of such leading U.S. municipal governments include Austin, TX; Boston, MA; Boulder, CO; Burlington, VT; Grand Rapids, MI; Madison, WI; Minneapolis, MN; New York, NY; Portland, OR; San Francisco, CA; Santa Monica, CA; and Seattle, WA. Some of the transitional changes invoked by these cities include requiring new municipal building projects to obtain LEED certification, purchasing a percentage of electricity from renewable sources, offering urban commuters a variety of mass transit options, and providing residents with numerous areas of green space and parks throughout the city.

One of the most potent opportunities for government to advance its own situation and that of the movement is in the area of bulk purchases of commonly used supplies. Governments procure and use voluminous amounts of white paper, cleaning supplies, street de-icing materials, and restroom products. With minimal training, some government purchasing agents stipulate their agency's preference for innocuous product choices from their suppliers and select the least-harmful affordable option for order. In even more mutually advantageous situations, collaborative municipal governments pool their orders to suppliers for these types of safer products and thereby enjoy deep volume discounts while actively supporting more intelligently designed bulk products. Today, sales representatives offering these products are well aware of the growing propensity for healthier and affordable products, and they pass along requests for additional types of supplies from clients to their company executives.

This type of mutually beneficial collaboration among governmental agencies is an advancement that emulates the cooperation-rich natural world. As distinct branches and levels of government develop deeper commitments to cooperation, more and more advantageous opportunities will surface and gradually come into practice. The improvements in our education systems will prepare government employees for recognizing intelligent and collaborative approaches for other operational issues. As we look to nature for additional opportunities to foster improved community relations, the quality of day-to-day government operations will slowly improve within the rising tide of sustainable business innovation.

In addition to governments forming partnerships with one another, some communities are finding value in multiple collaborations among governments, educational institutions, and private organizations. The concept of *community sustainability partnerships* has begun to develop in regions such as West Michigan where a university, two colleges, a city school system, and a city government have come together for the purpose of cooperatively restoring environmental integrity, improving economic prosperity, and promoting social equity throughout the region. Today, over 100 private, non-profit, governmental, and educational organizations have joined the regional coalition. This type of multi-sector alliance presents many crucial challenges for all parties involved, such as the contribution of appropriate representatives from each organization, the selection of an effective leadership team, the development of dependable funding strategies, the arrangement of formal meeting process and agenda items, the development of useful metrics to gauge the value production of each initiative, and the embedding of a component into a routine process that insures constant improvement of all operations through time. Other noteworthy partnerships located in Canada include the Alberta Urban Municipalities Sustainability Partnership and the New Communities of Tomorrow Partnership of Regina, SK.

Certainly the role of government is envisioned quite differently in sustainable business than it is by advocates of the modern environmental movement. Following the direction of sustainable business leaders inside the private sector, the most important role of government is to correct its policy incentives and disincentives, that is, to incentivize activities of business that produce only community value, and to disincentivize activities of business that discouraged members of our expanded concept of community. Another pressing movement reform target is the individual state corporate charter requirements, which, upon amendment, will favor locally owned and operated corporations that contribute more to their host communities than do traditional corporations. Finally, the slate of governmental reform measures includes the nature and scope of operational improvements that will allow government and its taxpayers to enjoy the benefits of the movement.

We now find ourselves at a point in our exploration of sustainable business where a thorough integration of movement components is useful. In the next chapter we will visualize how our upgraded businesses and organizations will coalesce and how life in our communities will change and improve for all of us when sustainable business principles are in full animation. Although such a conceptualization does require a fair amount of reader creativity and imagination, the next chapter will sharpen the reader's understanding of what to expect from the enormous amount of time and effort required for the changeover.

Guide Point 6: In addition to applying movement principles to its own operations, government's role in sustainable business is to craft economic policy incentives that support movement goals and policy disincentives that discourage counterproductive private sector behavior.

Chapter 7

Healthy, Beautiful, Diverse, and Durable

A common complaint by battle-hardened conventional business professionals is that the full purposes of sustainable business are too theoretical, abstract, and difficult to obtain. The 25-year business veteran of recessions, corporate bailouts, mergers, takeovers, and buyouts is usually more comfortable discussing cost-saving energy-efficiency improvements than conversions to sustainable energy systems. Furthermore, some appointed company sustainability leaders insist that high-minded sustainable business ideology, such as sun-powered energy sources, *products of service* closed-loop systems, natural-world emulation, and incentivizing locally owned business, is simply not practical or particularly important. Instead, these pragmatists say we should get our heads out of the clouds and concentrate on decreasing pollution and waste, which can save the company money.

This chapter takes a different approach to the paradigm-changing sustainable business phenomenon. In the next few pages, we project the sustainable business-influenced landscape three or four decades into the future. We will take a look at the intelligent and beautiful world that we can pass on to future generations, and in so doing, we sharpen the vision of our enduring intentions as evidenced by this unprecedented coalescence of business, modern society, and the natural world. The images and concepts of this sojourn are not simply our fantasy; rather, they embody the integrated positive results we can reasonably anticipate from the concerted efforts of all movement supporters. The chapter does set a high bar for humanity, challenging us to break out of our mundane, self-centered, and often cynical disposition and to explore another side of the human character alive in all of us.

159

For the short time it takes to read this chapter, you may want to find a comfortable chair in a quiet place, leave skepticism at the door, set your personal and professional concerns aside, and let your imagination work for you. Most of us do not often indulge in this sort of experience. As we actively engage in our day-to-day challenges and responsibilities, this type of activity may seem frivolous and difficult to justify. In our hearts, we may even be fearful of letting go of our cognitive reins in order to simply imagine. You may recall that my earlier requests for open-mindedness served you well, and again I suggest this approach in this chapter. When we finish this unit, you can expect a clearer and more complete understanding of the full ramifications of many years of applied sustainable business. You might even find yourself reflecting and envisioning the possibilities for humankind for the second half of the 21st century as well. So I encourage you now to take a deep breath, empty your mind of all presuppositions, and allow yourself to be led on a tour through an archetypal, but achievable, sustainable world.

7.1 Your Home

You have just pulled out a faded copy of *Fundamentals of Sustainable Business* from your bookcase and have decided to scan the pages. But these pages feel strange to you because nearly all hard copy books are now products of service, with light and silky polymer pages and extractable inks designed to cycle an infinite number of times. Your chair and many of your other leased home furnishings were manufactured inside your community and consist of some compostable and some technical material components. Your neighbor has worked many years for the company that provides much of your furniture and today holds an executive position. Your grandchildren often play with her grandchildren as both your older son and her daughter found stable and rewarding jobs in your beautiful hometown. You both serve on the neighborhood energy utility board, and you each invite the other's family over for dinner once every couple of weeks. The time spent together is as comfortable as an old shoe.

You set the book down now and decide to fix yourself some lunch. Your salad has fresh fruit and vegetables from your own garden and from the farmers' market that sets up twice a week within walking distance of your home this time of year. You set aside the kitchen waste for your backyard composter. The rich humus from this composter is used to fertilize your verdant vegetable and flower gardens. Every item in your home is either a product of service or a product of consumption, with surplus compost going back to the soil and obsolete technical materials safely stored in the garage for convenient weekly take-back and reprocessing. The meat and cheese in your sandwich were provided by the brother of one of your co-workers, and the bread was baked in your own home from a recipe of your sister-in-law who lives in another part of your city. The tea in your drink was grown in South Carolina and purchased at a local vendor's stand in the farmers' market. The water for the tea was provided by your municipal water supplier that uses ultraviolet light to eliminate pathogens and a dependable sand-filter system that removes minerals. Using chlorine to purify water was discontinued years ago, so the chronic risk of ingesting this carcinogen in drinking water and absorbing during your showers and baths were subsequently eliminated. Your electronics equipment, refrigerator, dishwasher, stove, and microwave oven are all leased products of service from regional companies, and the terms of the lease include all normal maintenance and repairs at no additional charge. You have the opportunity to trade in each model once a year for feature or appearance upgrades. No big-ticket purchases are busting your budget these days; instead, you make low, manageable monthly payments for all your products of service.

As you read anywhere inside your home during the day, you will feel as if you were outside because every room is illuminated by soft and diffused indirect lighting from the outdoors. Your many indoor plants thrive in this richly illuminated environment, providing additional indoor oxygen and humidity, absorbing your exhaled carbon dioxide, and softening indoor sounds with their beautiful flowers and leaves. The air inside your home is nearly as clean as the air outdoors since nearly all of the building materials, floor coverings, paints, and home furnishings do not contain volatile organic compounds. Your carpeting and rugs are made from safe product of consumption materials, so the abraded particles cause no harm to you or your family. The incidence of asthma in the general public has dropped dramatically since your college years because sensitive respiratory systems are subjected to much less deleterious material particles.

Surrounding the many exterior windows of your attractive, affordable, and strong geodesic home is a vegetative roof and imperceptibly blended photovoltaic surface material. The roof soil and vegetation help to insulate the inside temperature and buffer outside noises, which are mostly natural sounds since combustion engines for vehicles have been phased out. Little remains to paint on the exterior of most homes and the new vegetative roofs are projected to last over 50 years. Our urban landscaping is mostly native vegetation that requires no irrigation and little maintenance. Fertilizers and pesticides are no longer needed inside our cities as the indigenous vegetation is adapted for life in this particular region. Native plant landscaping also eliminates the runoff of toxic lawn and garden chemicals from our urban centers into our rivers, streams, lakes, and ground water, further reducing the cancer rate and pollution-related disease in the general population. The high cost of health care has been significantly lowered owing to the gradual removal of persistent toxins in our world, the decreasing stress levels we experience, and the emphasis on preventive health care practices.

Energy for your home is provided by a variety of sources. An inconspicuous PV system covers non-vegetative exterior surfaces and generates nearly all of your home's power needs during most days, with excess electricity used to charge an advanced product-of-service battery system capable of storing a week's worth of electricity for your home. When that storage system is full, additional electricity is used in an electrolysis process that cleanly produces hydrogen for your fuel-cell vehicle. A neighborhood utility company (you are a board member this year) sells solar- and wind-generated electricity to meet any remaining needs. On account of mechanical efficiency improvements and building design characteristics, the total energy consumption of your home is four to five times less than that of a similar home in 2009. Your sister who lives on the coast uses electricity generated by tidal and wave action, and the geothermal power facility founded by your brother and five other community members in Oregon has supported 200 other families for nearly 25 years.

7.2 Transportation

Ironically, the most effective transportation innovation may be the reorganization of the retail and residential landscape. In the sustainable future, you will find a locally owned grocery store, a hardware store, a drug store, three restaurants, and a general merchandise store within easy and safe walking distance from your home. You also have a park, tennis courts, and ball fields just a casual ten-minute stroll away. The emphasis on locally owned business by education and government policy incentives has set the stage for the development of walkable communities with farmers' markets, grocery stores, restaurants, bakeries, and specialty shops interspersed throughout the residential areas.

Your leased vehicle is powered by quiet and efficient electric motors and small dependable battery storage systems that are recharged as needed at home. The vehicle is also equipped with a series of small fuel cells that generate additional electricity after your batteries are drained. Your electric vehicle is comfortable, quiet, quick, clean, dependable, and affordable and has both product-of-service and product-of-consumption components. Your neighbor living behind you works at one of the many safe technical-nutrient cycling centers located in your community, which handles the product-of-service components of your vehicle, and he recently distinguished himself as the leading innovator at his facility.

Larger cities have convenient, clean, fast, comfortable, and affordable mass transit trains and buses that are propelled in a fashion similar to personal vehicles. Travel between cities and states is available by high-speed electric trains and hydrogen-burning aircraft (with water vapor being the only by-product). Ocean-going passenger and cargo ships have begun the transition to hydrogen-powered vessels.

Greenhouse gas emissions from transportation are nearly a thing of the past, and municipal transportation strategies capture most energy within their borders, which keeps billions of dollars churning inside local economies.

7.3 Your Retail Experience

It is time to meet your friends for dinner across town at one of your favorite restaurants. You and your spouse want to talk about college plans for your daughter and have decided to take the bus so that you both can devote full concentration to your conversation. On the leisurely five-minute walk from your doorstep to the bus stop, you greet at least a dozen other people you know sitting on their front porches or walking to various neighborhood destinations. As you quickly enter the bus (the transit card in your wallet or purse activates the fare charge), you find a seat, and briefly chat with more friends, then use the remaining travel time to discuss the college options for your high school-aged daughter. The bus driver remotely controls the intersection stop lights and uses the inside lane reserved only for mass-transit vehicles, so, even with stops, the bus makes the trip to the restaurant in about the same time as you would have in your electric car. You say goodbye to your friends and exit the bus within three blocks of your restaurant (local businesses now smartly locate along the popular bus and train routes with residential neighborhoods nearby). Without the need to find a parking spot and park your vehicle, you simply enter the restaurant relaxed and refreshed.

Inside the restaurant, you are cheerfully greeted by a hostess who recognizes you and your spouse from previous visits. Your friends have not yet arrived so you glance through a menu while you wait to be seated and see pictures and names of three local farmers that supply the fresh organically grown produce, meat, and dairy products for the eatery. Your spouse remarks that she works with the sister of one of the farmers whose mother and grandfather died fairly young of cancer, but so far, both the farmer and sister are cancer-free. As the staff prepares your table, you admire some of the beautiful artwork by local artists that is displayed at various locations throughout the restaurant. The smiling owner appears at the entrance area with a sample serving of still warm, made-from-scratch tapioca pudding for all the customers waiting for a table. As you taste the thoughtful and delicious offering, suddenly you and your spouse feel even more fortunate than those who already have been seated at their tables.

Your friends arrive and you are all seated along the window facing the bustling street. Glancing down at the menu, you hear your name spoken and look up to see the restaurant owner personally welcoming you to her establishment. She is lovingly carrying the smiling baby of a couple seated behind you, showing off the little tyke to all her patrons. The owner thanks you and your party for coming in, and after gently holding the baby for all to see, she leaves you to enjoy the meal. The fresh local food is delicious, the service genuinely friendly and prompt, and the time spent with your friends equally enjoyable. You have spent your entire evening out with friends in comfortable, attractive surroundings and have kept your money in the hands of other local citizens who will pass on the favor. You and your friends ordered two bottles of wine at dinner because you knew everyone would be riding home on the comfortable and convenient fuel-cell-powered city bus instead of driving.

Any food left on the tables is combined with scraps from food preparation and sent back to the farms that supply the restaurant. At the farm, the mix is composted and later added to the fields as fertile humus. With the elimination of monstrous hybrids (technical materials combined with consumable materials), human sewage is now a nearly pure compostable material. Sewage from the restaurant, other retail establishments, industry, and residential sources is now processed and composted at enhanced city sewage treatment plants, hauled back to farms, and spread onto the crop soil. No longer do sewage treatment plants deposit partially broken-down organic wastes into our surface water supplies, nor does agriculture systematically mine the soil of its fertility-providing nutrients. This process adds local jobs to the community, eliminates a major source of water pollution, and closes the loop on soil nutrients returning back to the farm field.

Selecting and purchasing your clothing is now a fresh and interesting experience. Shoppers enjoy a combination of the large selection and competitive pricing of the Internet and the personal service of a locally owned business. Most clothing stores are locally owned and function as outlets for dozens of different garment lines. These establishments typically keep only a modest amount of clothing inventory and floor space under their roofs, and the shopper orders from the Internet or from the clothing store itself. The outlets are also shipping hubs for the variety of clothing brands they represent. Light-weight package transport companies like United Parcel Service and Federal Express deliver individual clothing orders daily to the stores, while at the same time e-mail notices are sent telling shoppers that their orders are ready to be picked up. Shipping companies make a bulk delivery to one location a day sooner than if they had to individually travel to each customer's address, and shipping costs are lower because of the decreased delivery time and distance for each order. Rather than the shopper preparing and mailing return items, the outlet handles all refund and exchange procedures for each of the clothing companies it represents, which results in an added service for the buyer. Under this system, local outlet inventories remain modest, thereby further lowering costs, each local community hosts its own clothing retail center, and off-the-rack retail profits and a portion of the profits from Internet-ordered items remain in the local area. As in locally owned restaurants, these businesses locate along public transportation routes and develop long-lasting personal relationships with their customers. You now have a familiar face to address any issues concerning your retail experience, and successful store owners build a loyal and dependable customer base by providing friendly, convenient, and cost-effective retail clothing businesses.

Shopping for groceries has developed into quite a different affair compared to previous decades. You commute to a local farmers' market on your side of town where you make your way to your favorite vendors and select a variety of fresh fruits, vegetables, cheese and dairy products, bread, and meat. Occasionally, you might also buy jams, cider, sauces, syrups, soap, and even flowers from farmers that surround and support your city with healthy, organic, and locally grown and processed products. You ask a vendor the best apple choice for a cobbler you have planned to bake this afternoon. While you are leisurely browsing the market, you see many people you know and strike up a number of pleasant face-to-face conversations (not e-mail, cell phones, or instant messaging) that bring everyone up-to-date on commonly shared interests.

On the way home, you stop off at your neighborhood grocery store for some additional items not offered at the farmers' market. The store is owned by a corporation of community shareholders, so most of the operation's revenue stays inside your community. You live in a city with a population of 250,000, so various types of ethnic grocery stores are available throughout the urban area that provide a rich variety of product choices for many exotic cuisines. Even the grocery stores are designed for a pleasant and healthy customer experience with wonderfully diffused ambient daytime light, abundant fresh air, and safe interior materials and furnishings. Other grocery store features include indoor and outdoor composting vessels loaded with over-ripened or spoiling food, durable and re-usable shipping containers that have replaced cardboard and wooden shipping boxes and pallets, and a variety of sizes and shapes of reusable fabric grocery bags brought in by customers, some of which are manufactured by mentally challenged members of the community. Products within the store use a fraction of the packing and display materials of the past, with many sundries such as breakfast cereal, cookies, sugar, flour, soap, and detergents available for refill into reusable containers that customers bring back to the store at a discount.

In addition to local farmers providing local restaurants and markets with quality food products, these neighborhood grocery stores also have purchasing agreements with local farmers for as many products as they are available. In the northern regions of the U.S., most farmers have added a set of greenhouses that extend their growing season and increase crop production. Southern regions with fertile soils and longer growing seasons commonly export a small surplus of warm season crops to the northern domestic climes. We will examine the further development of sustainable agriculture later in this chapter.

Our product of service discussion in Chapter 2 provides us with a glimpse of our redesigned system of durable goods. Product-of-service dealerships in our towns and cities lease state-of-the-art appliances, electronics, and vehicles to their customers and act as take-back and repair agents for obsolete or malfunctioning items. Interestingly, the lease term on your personal vehicle will expire soon and so you have been comparing different models, contract options, and local dealerships over the Internet. After considering all the product features and lease terms, you sign a five-year product-of-service agreement for a new automobile that is fully assembled and will later be disassembled within your region and that sources more than 90% of its component parts in the U.S. (pre-leased vehicles are also available at a discount). You prepay your first six monthly payments and agree to bring the vehicle to the dealership for regularly scheduled complementary maintenance for the duration of the lease. You have the option to bring the vehicle back to the dealership at any sign of malfunction at no additional charge. Your insurance is also arranged through your dealership and the premiums are included in your lease payment. You have the option to upgrade or downgrade to another type of vehicle with predetermined price adjustments at any time during the duration of the lease. Only tires and fuel are your purchase responsibility for the tenure of the contract.

You drive away from the dealership propelled by four quiet and responsive electric motors, which are powered by electricity from an advanced series of battery and fuel-cell stacks. The only "waste products" during operation are pure water and some heat, which are used in the cooler months to warm the interior for the passengers. The vehicle releases no air pollution nor does it emit greenhouse gases, and the hydrogen used by the fuel cells to produce the electricity to run the motors comes from hydrolysis powered by sustainable energy. You produce most of the hydrogen for local travel during warm weather months at your home from the surplus of electricity produced from your personal energy-generation system (also a leased product of service) at your home. During the shorter days of winter, you purchase your hydrogen from local commercial filling stations. For interstate travel, you add hydrogen to your tank at commercial filling stations located across the entire country.

Your automobile has a combination of harmless biodegradable components (tires, breaking units, and interior materials) and sealed toxic technical-material components that make up the remaining portion of the vehicle. A breakthrough for bio-based tires and brake pads came from a scientific study of the natural world's approach to gradient changes in durable material chemistry. The technical-material components are perpetually owned by the manufacturing company, so they are engineered for continuous disassembly and cycling into new vehicle parts. Ironically, vehicles in the sustainable future are designed for an approximate seven-year road life. As transportation technology advancements are made, small and nimble product-of-service auto companies redesign models to embody the most recent improvements. The constant take back of technical vehicle components feeds the demand for production-line materials and nearly eliminates the extraction of virgin materials from sensitive regions of the planet.

Leasing products-of-service durable goods offers a number of advantages over sales agreements for customers, the dealership, the auto industry, and your greater community. For the customer, the amount of money spent per month on your personal vehicle is set for the period of the lease, routine repair and maintenance costs are made by the dealership, and your vehicle is kept in top running condition. Throughout the lease, if your needs change, you maintain the option to switch automobile types. Vehicle dealerships now cultivate long-term quality relationships with their patrons and maintain a sizeable customer base by focusing more on providing first-class service and less on advertising and marketing efforts for their products.

The U.S. automobile industry, which now assumes responsibility for sequestering all toxic materials used in its entire operation, cycles these technical materials continuously into new products, uses sustainable energy sources, is organized into trim region-supporting corporations, focuses on a stable domestic sales market, and has made the systemic changes necessary for lasting TTL durability. During the technology transition, salvageable materials from the huge conventional vehicle fleet were extracted, and monstrous hybrid components are being stored until new processes provide techniques for adding this material to the technical-nutrient cycle. An educated public now understands and appreciates the economic, environmental, and social value of this new approach to personal transportation and realizes that foreign automakers cannot provide such a total benefit package. The auto industry, along with other product-of-service business sectors and the communities in which they are located, also enjoys the lack of "boom-or-bust" demand cycles and the lasting prosperity and healthy living conditions that accompany this reform.

The numerous environmental perturbations from past transportation practices have all but disappeared. The elimination of these negative effects and the addition of green roofs and natural landscapes throughout the vehicle processing and production facilities have fostered a positive relationship with the natural world. The deep and constructive enhancements of durable goods provisioning have repositioned an important sector of our economy in order to put a crucial piece of the sustainable business mosaic in place.

7.4 Formal Education

In the sustainable future, from the first day of kindergarten to our terminal degree, we emphasize our connection with the natural world throughout our educational experience. Along with school buildings, books, desks, and computers, an outdoor natural classroom is considered an essential tool for every stage of public education. Prairies, woods, streams, and ponds are found adjacent to, or very near to, all schools and are regularly used for the study of the natural world. The natural world has become an indispensable pedagogical tool for environmental studies courses that are found in most grade levels. Beginning our investigation of nature at an early age is recognized as an enjoyable and useful step in building the foundation of a profound understanding and appreciation of the inner workings of the natural world.

The out-of-doors never leaves our curriculum as high school courses delve even deeper into natural connections of biology, history, economics, chemistry, business, sociology, physics, architecture, engineering, and geography. Classes are often taught by teams of teachers, with each blending one or more academic disciplines into the overall topic or theme of the exercise. Students are coached in various collaborative problem-solving and team-building exercises. One important goal is to recognize different team-member perspectives as strengths and to use the talents of all group members. Projects as divergent as designing a unique small business or creating a research methodology for a previously unanswered question provide interesting and engaging ways to develop creativity and innovation competency. The concept of *community well-being* is considered in every endeavor and exercise, and education is framed as a lifelong privilege and pleasure. Even students who choose not to attend college are given options for continuing a rewarding adult education process sponsored by various leading educational institutions in the region.

Your daughter will be graduating from high school this school year and is considering a number of colleges to attend in the fall. A variety of factors will enter into the decision. She learns that many colleges and universities require full-time students to work part-time for two semesters on campus. This practice lowers the tuition cost and fosters a deeper relationship between the college and the student. She sees that most college academic programs require students to complete a semester internship with an organization in their field of study during their junior or senior year. The intention of the internship requirement is to aid the student transition from the academic setting to the professional world. As your daughter looks over possible programs of study at a variety of colleges, she notices that the discipline of environmental studies is a part of nearly every interdisciplinary program. These environmental courses each have a field-based component or are a complete field course. Further investigation shows that at least one course on sustainability is a required part of the general studies curriculum for all students in all academic institutions.

Interestingly, a number of former college and university sustainable business departments have dropped the term "sustainable" from their official titles. Administrators explain this change by pointing out that sustainable business principles are the conventional approach to business in nearly all commercial endeavors and that there is no need to differentiate sustainable business from the simple term "business." In addition to the business course requirements for degrees in

business, core competencies in biology, chemistry, physics, communication, and environmental studies are standard parts of the program.
Business students in undergraduate programs also carefully examine
the dramatic and subtle relationships among business, the natural
world, and the human community.

7.5 Out on the Farm

On a trip to the countryside, you see many small family-owned farms
and ranches. The large and costly farm machinery of the past has
given way to compact and affordable hydrogen-powered walk-behind
tillers that work smaller acreages. Your young son has come along for
the ride today and notices the many butterflies and songbirds on the
rural landscape. Another interesting but subtle difference in rural
areas is the absence of bare soil. Exposed ground is vulnerable to soil
erosion and to sunlight that will harm the fertility-producing micro-
bial life found below the surface. Agricultural land is maintained with
a thick protective cover of dead plant material that prevents the deadly
ultraviolet radiation from penetrating the surface and that holds the
life-giving moisture in the soil much the same way that a prairie structures itself. The soil is commonly recognized as the most diverse and
rich natural community in the world and is treated accordingly; this
respectful treatment is a far cry from our past regard of farm ground
as a lifeless infrastructure for our food factories that must be prodded
into constant production.

Farmers have no need for expensive and harmful factory-
produced fertilizers and pesticides and have jettisoned that particular
cost component of production. Nearly all farms practice what in years
past was called "organic farming." That term is obsolete, as nearly all
successful farming operations use the organic, fertility-enriching techniques that have been constantly improved and expanded over the
past few decades. One of the most revolutionary developments for
sustainable agriculture has been the partnership with city governments that produces a constant supply of *humus* (a rich organic fertility-
providing component of the soil) for farmers. Cities and towns now
employ large-scale composting operations for their sewage and yard

waste that decompose and dry rich organic material and soil nutrients and makes them available to farmers and gardeners for incorporation back into the soil. The process simultaneously solves two of our more serious environmental problems: the need to return soil nutrients to the soil and the need to keep human waste material segregated from public water supplies. Interestingly, our industrial commitment to sequester all toxins in a closed-loop technical-material cycle has resulted in much more purified sewage and yard waste streams and has created the opportunity to safely return these valuable nutrients to our agricultural soils as fertilizers.

With the trend over the past few decades of urban residents, restaurants, and grocery stores buying as much of their food products as possible directly from local agriculture, most farmers have added a series of greenhouses to their farmsteads that provide a somewhat controlled climate and extend both ends of the growing season. In the middle and northern regions, greenhouses allow all seedlings to germinate earlier in the spring as well as add a month or two to the fall growing season for full-time greenhouse plants. The field of *hydroponics* (growing crops in nutrient solutions without soil to provide support) has expanded and allows many of the greenhouses to flourish on a year-round basis. Continuing on your drive, you spot a number of farms located near heat-producing industrial operations; these farms have partnered with the factories to use previously wasted heat to warm their adjacent greenhouses throughout the entire winter. Reciprocally, the factory lunchrooms now feature delicious supplies of fresh fruits and vegetables from the farms for their staff during the entire year.

Your grandfather who has come along for the ride in the back seat comments that these farm fields look quite different than the ones in his generation. He notes how many more perennial crop (produce yields from the same plant root structure year after year) fields exist now than in the past. In addition to traditionally perennial nut trees, fruit trees, strawberries, asparagus, and grapes, you see other perennial strains of wheat, beans, rye, corn, and tomatoes on your drive. One major advantage of perennial crops for farmers is the elimination of the time and expense required to plow, cultivate, and replant each year. Another important benefit is the elimination of soil erosion and the soil sterilization caused by reworked soil that is directly exposed to the wind and sun. Still another advantage is the opportunity to install ultra-efficient underground trickle-drip irrigation systems when necessary and leave them in the ground throughout productive years of the perennial plant stock.

Perhaps the most surprising agricultural practice noticed by your grandfather is *polyculture farming*, which involves growing four or five compatible crops together in the same field at the same time. When you inquire about the success of this relatively new strategy with a local farmer (actually polyculture farming was practiced by a number of pre-Columbian agrarian societies of the Americas[19]), she remarks that losses from insects and plant disease have been lower in polyculture fields and that new *cultivars* (plant types used in agriculture) are being developed to expand the choice of crop combinations. Candidates for these new cultivars come from native species found naturally in the same region. Polyculture farming is a *biomimetic innovation* that embeds prairie-like community-member diversity into our sustainable farming endeavors. Most of the harvesting of polyculture crops is still done by hand but industrial engineers are beginning to design simple machinery that will lighten the work load of polyculture farmers.

On your drive back home, you notice farms and ranches within a few miles of the city that not only provide food for urban customers but also capture wind and solar power that supplements community energy needs. Surpluses of both electricity and hydrogen are produced by these small farm- and ranch-based operations and are then transported to a variety of industrial customers that do not produce all of their energy needs on site. Company officials appreciate the opportunity to buy clean energy from local suppliers, and the farmers and ranchers are grateful for the additional source of revenue.

---

[19] See Rebelloto *et al.* (2008) for an insightful analysis of pre-Columbian polyculture practices.

7.6 Your Workplace

Visualizing all of the changes in our world that were described earlier in the chapter might seem overwhelming. In fact, some people may find it hard to believe that such an enormous amount of change is even possible in only three or four decades. If you are old enough, you may want to think for a moment about the difference in the world today and the world a generation ago, without Internet, e-mail, computers, or cell phones. In the 1970s and 1980s, we anticipated much value coming from these changes, we embraced the technological advances, and then we made this technology a part of our lives. Next, you could consider how drastically industry shifted in just a few short months after our nation entered World War II. During that tumultuous period, we perceived our adversaries as a grave threat to our very existence and immediately converted domestic industrial product lines to weapons and wartime goods in order to defeat our enemies. Certainly, our current problems of business pose a quite different threat than a geopolitical world war, but the grave situation outlined in Chapter 1 nonetheless remains a formidable challenge. Although the movement innovations described so far in this chapter are impressive and represent two additional generations of commitment to TTL progress, you may find the following description of your workplace experience similarly dramatic and consequential.

Considering your growing expertise in the movement, you may have expected your place of employment to use energy only from sustainable sources — the sun, wind, Earth (geothermal), and ocean. During your work shift today, your parked-but-functioning fuel-cell vehicle is plugged into your company's energy system, and you are selling your company electricity generated by your vehicle. Your company is also purchasing a portion of its energy from the small-scale wind and solar production facilities on nearby farms. Designed similarly to your home, your company building surfaces are combinations of vegetative surfaces and photovoltaic material that generates clean daytime electricity for your company. Even the energy-capturing exterior building surfaces are effective products of service that are regionally manufactured and reprocessed using sustainable energy and do not contribute toxic materials to the biosphere. All of the energy used on your worksite is produced within a 25-mile radius of the building and supports the stable prosperity of your local community.

Another noteworthy change from the past is the location and distribution of the homes and businesses of our communities. Industrial facilities are not as separated from residential areas or from retail operations as compared to three or four decades ago. Although some groups of businesses that have collaborative relationships do tend to locate together, the spatial distribution of residential, retail, and industrial activities is becoming less segregated and more integrated. The term *industrial beauty* is not an oxymoron any longer; local business owners take pride in the architecture, landscaping, and elegance they provide to the whole community. With attractive locally owned business, the absence of industrial toxins, and clean and quiet vehicles, the need for residential, industrial and retail zoning restrictions is disappearing. Like the woods behind your house, our communities are now evolving into appealing mixtures of healthy and beautiful storefronts, production facilities, and homesites. Natural communities effectively integrate all these activities in the same location, and we have begun to do the same.

An interesting feature of business is that *synergistic associations* among various types of companies are quite common. This context of synergism refers to an interaction of discrete organizations that produces greater results than the sum of the individual organizations acting independently. As you drove to work, you noticed a truck from another business accepting materials left over from your company's manufacturing operations that fill the need of the other business quite well. Companies joined together in large cooperatives will often influentially petition suppliers to develop new products that deliver more TTL value to their operations. Brokering this type of mutually beneficial arrangement via electronic or face-to-face meetings is common for cutting-edge businesses, and such agreements improve the situations of all the parties involved as well as the local community. Movement leaders in the private sector recognize the long-term benefits of fluid regional communication and collaboration for simultaneously solving the challenges of multiple local businesses.

The personal reputation of business owners and the professional relationships developed among company leaders are even more important than they were in the recent past; many lasting agreements are first made by a handshake or by the word of those involved. Furthermore, thriving and durable regional economies are continuously monitored and upgraded by their members, and the myriad of ongoing mutually beneficial partnerships is now a mainstream business practice. Competition among other companies in your sector is still an important part of business, but the rules of engagement are to *strive together* for the newly defined concept of TTL excellence. Similar to how a variety of superior eating establishments make up a successful restaurant district, groups of other similar businesses have learned to appreciate one another's contributions to economic stability.

Another interesting business development involves the transparency, distribution, and flow of information inside your company. Specialized computer software organizes, displays, and provides access to a full complement of operational information for all permanent company employees. Except for proprietary or confidential personnel data, all staff may access and examine the complete set of company files. All electronic communications inside the company are now instantly labeled, time-dated, summarized, and organized into specific topic folders by software, and these "community" electronic topic folders are conspicuously computer displayed and available to employees from all departments. This type of fluid and multi-directional information pathway is common inside organizations, enabling staff working in one area to keep up-to-date with all areas and activities of the company. Employees are aware of the full array of situations involving the company, so individual decisions are more appropriate and fitting for the entire organization.

The hierarchical organization of your company is quite flat, with many impactful decisions made by the employee team most involved with the specific situation. Waiting for approval of your decision from a distant supervisor is a thing of the past. Quality education, sound hiring procedures, appropriate working environments, and fair compensation arrangements have led to competent people being hired throughout the organization, so providing them the opportunity to make decisions on issues within their immediate purview is both an effective and efficient use of the talented company work force. All professionals are held to high standards of performance, but the stifling layers of administrative bureaucracy are gone in most organizations. Company professionals share the belief that the purpose of their organization is to serve their clients and the entire community, and all staff members are encouraged to use their talents and those of their team members to the best of their abilities.

The decades of deep systemic improvements and long-term planning is paying big dividends. Crisis management, common in many organizations just two generations ago, is rare. Organizations have *cyclical improvement processes* embedded in their DNA. Part of day-to-day operations includes processes that systematically improve TTL value production over time. Taking our lead from nature's ability to adapt to a changing set of environmental circumstances, staffs of organizations spend portions of each day reviewing current processes, anticipating changing business conditions, and designing appropriate amendments in processes for the coming weeks and months. Recognizing the competitive advantage of continually improving its standard of community service, a business acknowledges and rewards creative and meaningful process innovation by employees, who regularly monitor, assess, and improve how their company executes its TTL business.

As an example, your company has recently expanded its ties with the local college in your community and has doubled its number of business internships (only a few years ago referred to as sustainable business). Company employees find that the fresh and unbiased perspectives of interns have generated valuable TTL suggestions, improving parts of the operations that were previously overlooked. The experience is equally rewarding for the business, students, and community. A specific discovery made via your company's commitment to constant improvement was to mix the composting materials from your operation with the composting materials from the adjacently located business to the south. The different types of composting materials now combine to form even richer, more complete and more valuable fertilizer material than either company had been producing alone. This collaboration is another example of businesses helping each other by establishing a *synergistic connection in operations*. Nature's industrial infrastructure has flourished from this sort of collaboration for billions of years, and now human industry is beginning to reap the benefits of such alliances.

Refined sustainability metric systems, now in place inside nearly all companies, effectively measure and track the TTL progress for various parts of the operation as well as the entire organization itself. The metric system inside your company has been evolving and improving for many years, and one of your work team's accomplishments has been to further improve the system. This afternoon, your company is hosting the second in a series of conferences attended by over 60 area business representatives for the purpose of designing a single metric system to effectively monitor the activities of all the businesses in attendance. A single system used by all would allow meaningful long-term performance-score comparisons among organizations. You are scheduled and prepared to guide the proceedings and facilitate the discussion.

If our workplace tour has your head spinning, your feet tiring, and your stomach growling, then we will take a break. Looking around, we see containers of chilled fresh fruit and vegetables, yogurt, fruit juices, and water that are provided for employees during their work day. The cafeteria, adjacent to the company day-care facility for infants, children, and geriatrics, has a complete menu of fresh, healthy, and delicious foods available to all employees as part of their compensation package. A complementary massage therapist is available without an appointment for 15-minute sessions from 10:00 a.m. until 2:00 p.m. during each work day. You walk by the comfortable recliners available for napping as needed by employees on their breaks. Walking and running trails wind through the natural areas surrounding the facility. Plenty of comfortable sitting locations are scattered about outside for individuals or groups to eat lunch, catch up on everyday life with a colleague, or simply to enjoy the weather. A huge sunroom just off the cafeteria provides a comfortable gathering place during all types of weather, with shade panels available to provide a cool area to relax during the warmer days.

Does this work environment sound too extravagant to be practical? Successful companies of the future take great care to hire the best employees available and to provide a comfortable and healthy work environment. Keeping valuable and talented employees on staff and providing a productive, relaxed, and creative work atmosphere for them are critical components of a sustainable business. The companies with a reputation for strongly supporting their employees tend to attract the most qualified applicants when a position comes open. Along with the benefits and perks, these companies have exceptionally high performance standards for their employees, with mandatory probationary periods helping to determine the most promising candidates. The base pay for nearly all employees is somewhat low, but TTL production incentives provide the opportunity for all staff who excel to earn a very attractive total compensation package.

Your company, like most other successful businesses, only rarely adds facilities or expands its workforce. Many of the systemic changes of the sustainable business revolution, such as leasing durable goods, refocusing on regional markets, and supporting locally owned companies, have helped stabilize the untenable expansion and contraction of the business sector. With TTL goals and long-term considerations helping to guide decisions, business leaders are choosing to continually improve the performance of existing facilities and expand only after carefully considering the long-term effect on local communities. Intelligent economic growth is recognized as an *intensification of TTL value production* inside established operations and is monitored by a re-tooled set of economic indicators that measure value produced rather than simply the output of goods and services. This ideology is quite a change from the past belief that business and a healthy economy must constantly expand with new operations and increased production output and sales.

Thus far, we have become familiar with the root problems of business, considered the natural world as a guide for meaningful change, discussed the vital components of the movement to date, learned about a variety of organizations that now apply movement theory to practice, summarized the roles of both education and government, and imagined life in the middle of the new millennium after a series of purposeful and intelligent systemic changes by business and community. Hopefully by this point, many of us are now getting our arms around the nebulous conception of sustainable business. The last chapter will describe some serious obstacles and threats to the continuing progress of the movement and proffer some suggested remedies for these formidable challenges that have appeared on the horizon.

Guide Point 7: A growing mainstream commitment to sustainable business principles has begun to transform our communities in a myriad of delightful and healthy ways that significantly raise our quality of life and strengthen our future.

Chapter 8

Falling Off the Log

After our glimpse into the sustainable future in Chapter 7, we now return to the present and consider the movement's current situation in its entirety. The numerous positive developments up to this point notwithstanding, sustainable business is still in its infancy. In order to reach full maturity, this movement must navigate some rough waters that hold a collection of rip tides and whirlpools. Much of this final chapter is devoted to identifying and discussing these obstacles to the sustainable business movement and suggesting some appropriate solutions. It is important that we recognize and acknowledge these barriers to progress; only then can we become part of the answers to these problems. Ironically, we have brought on many of these threats ourselves, and potent solutions to them require that we understand, accept, and vigorously confront them.

8.1 Recognizing the Threats

The earlier chapters have summarized the serious environmental and social dilemmas that have accompanied our industrial efforts into the 21st century. Many of these dire consequences, such as pollution-induced illness, birth defects, an increasing incidence of cancer deaths, high unemployment, diminishing quality of life, reduced opportunities for future generations, and spiraling industrial production costs, are often considered unavoidable "facts of life" and are often not associated with poor industrial design choices. Our collective responses to these unfortunate experiences have been shortsighted attempts to ameliorate the symptoms while often not recognizing the underlying systemic sources of the problems. Unfortunately, this symptomatic approach currently dominates our formal research efforts, media coverage, and educational systems. For example, we often unwittingly view the tragedy of a three-year old girl with brain cancer as the lack of a cure for her condition, rather than as our collective failure to recognize and change the basic approach of established and respected energy and material provisioning practices.

Society's prolonged collective *ignorance* concerning the complete story of how industrial practices affect our quality of life today and in the future presents a sizeable barrier to effective sustainable business advancement. Indeed, we are only able to fix something if we know not only that it is broken, but also *how* it is broken. Unfortunately, as discussed in Chapter 5, our current formal educational system fails to prepare us to ask intelligent questions and to recognize the insidious and endemic problems of business. Not surprisingly, the direction taken for gathering valuable information by much of our academic and private researchers reflects this same ignorance and lack of comprehensive perspective. A cure for cancer is insignificant when compared to the removal of the anthropogenic root causes for that same cancer, but unfortunately, the preponderance of our efforts to deal with cancer do not reflect this reality.

Clearly, a significant threat to the movement is the powerful bastion of ignorance that we perpetuate and allow to handicap our progressive efforts. Each of us has the opportunity to confront this obstacle, to dismantle its inefficacious attributes, and to move us closer to intelligent living. The redesigned formal education system proposed in Chapter 5 has the capability to deliver the social infrastructural foundation required to eliminate this barrier to lasting prosperity. Similar to our other positive cultural adaptations through-out history, such as offering a public education for all citizens, this change in approach to learning will provide greater opportunities to continue our movement forward.

8.2 Opportunistic or Altruistic

Perhaps the most formidable threat for the expansion and intensification of the sustainable business movement is the *inherent desire of each person to accommodate his or her own basic needs*. Although the ability of man to work together in social groups has proven extraordinarily beneficial, nearly all individuals still possess an intensely strong instinct to satisfy his or her own requirements for survival. Indeed, Garrett Hardin, a distinguished University of California human ecology professor, believes the modest longevity of our species on Earth is due in no small part to the strongly prevailing urge of an individual, when confronted with a choice, to nearly always act in his or her own self interest. Hardin points out in his seminal 1968 journal article, *The Tragedy of the Commons,* that throughout humankind's tenure on Earth, individuals with this instinct held a distinct survival advantage compared to those more selfless individuals, lived a longer reproductive life, and were more likely to pass on this genetic-controlled trait to their offspring. He says that, because of our genetic heritage, we will most often act in our own self-interest. Our actions may also benefit others consequentially, but until we have met our needs, we will not make choices the vast majority of the time that specifically meet the needs of others.

The relevance of this self-centered human characteristic for sustainable business lies in the role that ethics play in deepening our commitment to the movement. Initially, however, most business people are attracted to the movement by the opportunity for significant cost-saving and the positive publicity for their business. The identification of "low-hanging fruit" in the form of simple cost-effective waste-reduction opportunities captures the early attention of executives. At some point, however, when leaders seriously ponder the TTL concept, ethical considerations enter into the decision of whether to raise the level of commitment. Even though sustainable business practices do deliver economic benefits for the participating organization, significant effort is spent integrating natural world and human world benefits into operations as well. Our continual investment into maintaining healthy communities that provide the bedrock for prosperity is indeed, at least in part, a selfless act. Whether or not we embrace and empathize with the natural world and other living humans, our TTL efforts involve significant benefits for many other humans and wild creatures in our world.

Leaders overwhelmingly driven to act only in their own best interests will find little reason to deeply involve their companies in authentic TTL sustainable business. If the vast majority of conventional business people are, in fact, hardwired opportunists, then the business pool from which we can attract new members to the movement shrinks dramatically, as do the chances for sustainable business to reach its fruition. On the other hand, relatively small motivated groups of individuals have periodically led notable societal change throughout the ages, such as the emergence of many major religions or the signing of the *Magna Carta* in Medieval Europe. The extent to which basic human self-centeredness threatens sustainable business remains to be seen, and movement leaders are wise to be mindful of this possible threat.

8.3   An Aversion to Risk

One commonality among most captains of industry today is a deep-seated aversion to risk in matters involving the operation of their company. They remind us that guiding an organization through difficult economic times is fraught with uncertainty, and any opportunity to reduce unnecessary risk must not be ignored. Indeed, a retreat to more conservative business tactics during a tumultuous business cycle is normal and often reasonable. Staying clear of dangerous and avoidable situations is arguably the only rational approach to an unpredictable future.

Another perspective that also warrants consideration during these times is the importance of recognizing potent but ephemeral opportunities that present themselves. Standing strategically pat in tough times can amount to painting oneself into an even smaller corner, especially if avenues exist to better the situation. An economic downturn is all the more reason to remain open to substantial positive change, even when the element of risk is attached. Chances are your competitors are faced with similar situations and choices, and the organization that makes the most of opportunities during the challenging times will distinguish itself in its field, just as cream rises to the top of the milk pail.

Risk is a powerful motivator in business. The possibility of injurious consequences often brings up strong feelings of fear and angst that are difficult to set aside. The systemic change that accompanies authentic sustainable business principles and practices does carry risk for organizations and businesses. Whether or not this associated risk will significantly stall movement progress remains to be seen. An anecdotal survey, however, of the organizations that have already begun serious transition efforts and the value these innovations have generated suggest that the competitive advance enjoyed far outweighs the accompanying risk. Indeed, the most dangerous choice for business and individuals may well be to ignore the opportunities that sustainable business presents and to allow our aversion of risk to control our destiny.

8.4 The Overwhelming Cost

Another particularly stout barrier for continued movement advancement is the financial cost of developing the requisite technical knowledge and infrastructure advancements that would accompany such progress. Some examples include improved battery technology, hydrogen-generation facilities and distribution systems, products of service take-back and disassembly processes, ocean-derived energy systems, photovoltaic advancements, retirement of the fossil-fuel infrastructure, and improvements in material chemistry. If considered in aggregate, the necessary changes are quite overwhelming and could be viewed by skeptics as a reason to justify abandoning the revolution. But when considered from the following perspective, the transition will present itself as much more manageable.

Today, the level of ongoing technological research and development is impressive and involves dozens of nations and hundreds of companies.[20] The substantial payoff for successful sustainable business-related research has been demonstrated by numerous companies, with some selected examples included in Chapter 4. The current trend of increasing investment in sustainable technology will address many of

---

[20] See King (2004) for a comprehensive review of international technology research efforts.

the critical needs for maintaining the momentum of movement transition. The success of these research and development projects will hopefully attract even more venture capital into the movement in a manner similar to the series of events that led to a significant increase in the number of domestic uses for petroleum products after World War II. The potential payoff for revolutionary technical discoveries is very high.

A further important consideration concerning the total cost of the movement is that appropriate technological innovation will be spread across time. One common practice today among movement-involved organizations is to use the cost savings from efficiency improvements to fund deeper process development. Continuing to reinvest the financial earnings from current technology into further improvements delivers a cascading and positive effect on movement momentum. Considering the ancient Chinese proverb by Confucius, "A journey of a thousand miles begins with a single step," we now find ourselves the first few rewarding miles down the road of technological development for the sustainable business revolution, and it is reasonable to assume that continuing the trip will be just as fruitful. This immense economic and technological challenge loses much of its overwhelming and crippling effect when considered from the combined perspective of our early success stories, the research and development programs already in place, and a prioritized TTL investment schedule across decades in the future. Throughout our tenure on Earth, human society has overcome a wide variety of sizeable threats. Our greatest strength as a species has been our ability to behaviorally adapt to threatening conditions, and we have no reason to lose our resolve in this current global challenge.

8.5 Indecent Exposure

Although imitation may be the sincerest form of flattery, the practice of impersonating legitimate sustainable business organizations, products, or services is anything but adulation for the movement. The term *TTL value fraud* refers to the practice of misleading customers about the TTL benefits of a company's activities, products, or services. In this scam, customers are promised a higher quality environmental or social benefit or both from a particular product or service than they actually receive, with the culpable organization taking credit as a genuine movement participant. Perpetrators use a variety of disingenuous tactics to accomplish TTL value fraud and thus do the movement the significant injustice of misrepresenting authentic sustainable business. The following are five of the more common *TTL value fraud* practices today.

The Concealed Compromise occurs when a product, service, or organization claims it is "sustainable" based on one or two positive attributes, while many other seriously negative environmental and social characteristics are concealed. Companies that use this form of deception often provide less value than others that make no TTL claims at all. An example of such a company is an office paper manufacturer that advertises its cycled paper as "eco-friendly," while using a chlorine bleaching process that emits dioxin compounds to extract the inks from the used paper. Another case in point is the corporate-owned department store that claims to be a heart-of-the-movement sustainability practitioner owing to a smattering of less-harmful energy-efficiency practices, while hiring mostly part-time employees at minimum wage to avoid paying the higher wages and health benefits offered to full-time employees. An educated public sector that requires business practice transparency and chooses other more appealing retailing options is often the best defense against this type of marketing. Ultimately, it is customer demand that determines the ultimate success of companies, and the movement-sophisticated customers (the numbers are ever increasing) who avoid these types of pretender organizations and patronize authentically transitioning companies will determine the successful players on the retail landscape.

A second tactic, *The Unsubstantiated Claim*, refers to a publicized beneficial environmental or social feature of a product, service, or organization that provides customers no method to check the authenticity of the assertions. Reputable companies with nothing to hide routinely provide sources of verification to the curious shopper on the product packaging, on an insert, or on its Website. Unsubstantiated claims are often made indiscriminately with no supporting evidence in existence. An example of this form of TTL value fraud is the assertion that a shirt is made from all organic materials and that no sweat-shop labor was used in its production, with no third-party organization or specific accessible information verifying either of these claims. Furthermore, even a letter of inquiry receives only the hollow reply that this information is proprietary and unavailable for public inspection. A concerned customer's next move could be a follow-up communiqué stating that without verification of the claims of the company, he or she will not purchase any of the company's products in the future but will pass on the questionable practices of the company to family and friends.

A third scheme to mislead consumers involves describing a product or service with a term implying some sort of environmental or social benefit that is ambiguous, unclear, and without relevant definition. This *Vagueness of Claim* occurs when using the words "green" or "all-natural" to describe a product in a way that carries some positive connotation, but the exact meaning of the terms varies from customer to customer. Because these terms mean different things to different people, this common marketing tactic removes the company's responsibility to meet a standard for these descriptive terms, but the company can claim a significantly positive TTL characteristic at the same time. For instance, a company makes the decision to advertise one of its cleaning products as "green," and the only distinguishing characteristic is a 50% reduction of one of several problematic ingredients. Another example is a body lotion that purports to contain only "all-natural" ingredients. The term *natural* might be construed to mean existing without human intervention or made from materials found only in nature, but in either case, "natural materials" could be harmful to us and do not guarantee the safety or effectiveness of the lotion. An educated and discerning consumer is the best defense against this marketing tactic. If these veiled attempts fail to persuade an informed and thoughtful public, organization leaders will eventually be pushed to concede that much more is needed to be recognized as an authentic movement participant.

A fourth technique used to deceive the public is to attach a claim to a product or service that implies importance but simply makes no difference and has no relevance to the customer. An example of this type of *Claim Irrelevance* is a termite control company that today advertises itself as "Dieldrin-free," when dieldrin, a virulent pesticide, has been banned in the U.S. for termite control since 1987. Carbon-neutral chewing gum is another case of associating a term having an environmentally positive meaning (carbon-neutral) with a completely unrelated product. Even if the gum was manufactured and packaged using a process that did not add any carbon to the atmosphere, producing and delivering the ingredients to the production plant and transporting the gum to its retail centers would generate considerable carbon emissions from our petroleum-based transportation systems. The carbon-neutrality of chewing gum is irrelevant to the environmentally conscious consumer and has no legitimacy when deceptively used in the marketplace.

A final and audacious method that unscrupulous organization leaders employ that qualifies as TTL value fraud is to *Make False Claims* for the purpose of projecting the illusion that their company is a sustainable enterprise. Using advertising campaigns or Websites to display and disseminate patently untrue operational features or characteristics, some companies attempt to associate themselves with the positive publicity of the sustainable business movement, while maintaining conventional business practices. Other businesses guilty of this duplicity are incapable of joining the movement because of the nature of their activities, such as oil companies and chemical manufacturers.

As mentioned above, a consumer well-educated in sustainable business principles will recognize TTL value fraud and may communicate to company officials how it has have caused the loss of their patronage. Perceptive journalists and the broadcast media have the opportunity to expose these practices in their work. Further, government legislators have the opportunity to amend truth-in-advertising regulations that discourage such machinations. However, the ultimate responsibility for honest and ethical advertising and marketing practices rests with the company officials that decide such matters. Hopefully, as the movement matures and becomes even more influential and as our education systems evolve, even business people engaged in this dark-side behavior will begin to recognize the long-term advantages of authentic sustainable business.

8.6 Pretenders and Emasculators

Business leaders in today's difficult economic environment often find themselves deeply rutted in a crisis-management style that moves from symptom to symptom of deeper systemic problems, putting out one operational fire and moving on to the next. Unfortunately, this strategy does produce immediate gratification for management in the form of reduced fallout, and the sources of these symptomatic effects are never corrected. This type of short-sighted mindset seduces some decision-makers into attempting an expeditious capturing of movement benefits by means of the TTL value fraud tactics outlined in the previous section. This practice not only harms customers of the misrepresented companies but also threatens the sustainable business movement itself. As these pretender companies attempt to blend into the authentic movement landscape, curious members of the public may be unable to discern the authentic transitioning organization from the pretender company. These opportunistic companies are often well-funded and have large advertising budgets from which to perpetuate their sustainable business myth. The public commonly evaluates the meaningfulness of the entire movement through the impressions given by these types of shallow but visible promotions. The danger exists in this scenario for the inquiring public sector to misjudge the essence of the movement and to dismiss sustainable business as an insignificant passing fad.

In an attempt to attract recognition as a movement leader, these pretender organizations sometimes sponsor sustainable business conferences or events, pairing with other pretenders and often using a combination of the TTL value fraud tactics previously discussed. These events are branded as movement-based, offer questionable agendas, and have the effect of diluting and misrepresenting sustainable business to an even larger audience. Adding to the confusion, media coverage of these events is generally carried out by reporters ill-prepared to appropriately represent and critique the proceedings. Their public accounts normally reflect the narrow message of the organizers and lack the poignant reality that lies beneath the surface of the prepared press releases.

In this section, we have discussed different sources that broadcast misinformation and misrepresent the legitimate TTL concepts and infrastructure. These oversimplified and deficient versions of labeled sustainable business more closely align with conventional business and portray the movement as a mere shell of its essence. Our hefty charge is to do our best to honor and protect the salient ingredients of current credible sustainable business thought, while keeping our minds open through time to recognize other priceless additions that will contribute more substance to the movement.

Any one of the threats discussed in this chapter has the capability to seriously stall the movement's progression, and a collection of threats could completely derail the coalescence. However, if movement leaders recognize the extent of danger inherent in each obstacle, make a decision to counter each threat as effectively as possible, and then collaboratively design and implement a plan for each threat, the chance of intensifying movement progress and achieving success increases significantly. We now have the opportunity to support continued progress and to collectively dissolve these impediments that stand in our way.

In this challenge, as with all others in the sustainable business revolution, inspiring and visionary leadership is essential at all levels of engagement. Whether conversing with a fellow worker about a particular sustainable topic or giving a talk on the national lecture circuit, each of us involved in the movement has his or her own opportunities to provide leadership to advance sustainable business thought and to reduce the threats that are before us. The success enjoyed thus far is due in large part to the grassroots participation by many people in many places around the globe; continued success is perhaps even more dependent upon informed, thoughtful, and motivated people adding their personal contributions as the opportunities arise.

8.7 Six Essential Characteristics

As we gradually integrate the concepts, values, and broad implications of sustainable business into our personal and professional lives, most of us will discuss this new body of knowledge with many people from various walks of life. During these conversations, our contentions will be challenged and debated, so the ability to draw from a concise but comprehensive set of characteristics that represent the essence of the movement will be key to elucidating such a discussion. The following list includes six essential characteristics of mature and authentic sustainable business:

Triple Top-line Value Production

The TTL establishes three *simultaneous requirements* of sustainable business activities — financial benefits for the company, natural world betterment, and social advantages for employees and members of the local community — with each of these three components recognized as equal in status.

Nature-Based Knowledge and Technology

This biomimicry-based principle involves the conscious emulation of natural-world genius in terms of growing our food, harnessing our energy, constructing things, conducting business, healing ourselves, processing information, and designing our communities.

Products of Service to Products of Consumption

Products of service are durable goods routinely leased by the customer that are made of technical materials and that are returned to the manufacturer and re-processed into a new generation of products when they lose their usefulness. *Products of consumption* are shorter-lived items made only of biodegradable materials that are broken down by detritus organisms after the products lose their usefulness. This principle requires that we manufacture only these two types of products and necessitates the gradual but continual reduction of products of service and their replacement with products of consumption as technological advancements allow.

Solar, Wind, Geothermal, and Ocean Energy

This principle advocates employing only sustainable energy technology — solar, wind, geothermal, and ocean — that can meet our energy needs indefinitely without negative effects for life on Earth.

Local-Based Organizations and Economies

This ingredient includes durable, beautiful, and healthy communities with locally owned and operated businesses and locally managed non-profit organizations, along with regional corporations and shareholders working together in a dense web of partnerships and collaborations.

Continuous Improvement Process

Operational processes inside successful organizations include provisions for constant advancement and upgrade as the company does its business. The continuous process of monitoring, analyzing, redesigning, and implementing is used to intensify TTL value production as conditions change and new opportunities emerge.

8.8 International Implications

This section includes a limited discussion of the relationship between sustainable business and two international topics — globalization and developing nations. Numerous articles and books have been written about the effects of globalization on business as well as sustainable development initiatives inside developing nations. A thorough and in-depth discussion of sustainable business in the context of these international topics would require another complete and separate book. The following remarks are purposely limited to specific issues within these international topics.

Globalization, in an economic context, refers to an increasingly integrated global economy characterized especially by free trade, free flow of capital, and the use of low-priced foreign labor markets. This set of economic conditions has been cultivated and supported since the end of World War II by various political leaders around the globe for the purpose of advancing the general prosperity and increasing the interdependence of nations so as to deter another major global conflict. Long lists of positive and negative economic, environmental, and social results of globalization have been authored by a variety of economists, environmentalists, and social advocates. Although an international anti-globalization movement has surfaced, many scholars feel that globalization is an increasingly persistent set of conditions that will intensify throughout this century.

In contrast, the sustainable business movement, as envisioned in this text, embraces the continued development of inter-connected, community-supporting regional and local economies. Imports and exports, both out of the region and out of the country, will be part of a sustainable economy; however, the majority of natural resources and markets for goods and services will be anchored inside the local and regional communities. A local economy that primarily relies on regional markets and natural resources gives stability to a community and provides the capacity to better influence favorable economic conditions inside its region. Growth in these markets will be more dependent on an *intensification of local value delivery*, rather than an insatiable quest for expanding into new markets. Moreover, sustainable regional economies will result in a *significant reduction in the cross-continental character of the global economy* and in an increased diversification of local economies. Today, some macro-economists consider the sustainable business movement too trivial to influence the global economy in such a profound way. However, a lack of clear understanding and appreciation of the nature, distribution, and scope of the sustainable business revolution contributes to these conclusions.

Sustainable development inside developing nations (where economies are dominated by subsistence agriculture) has been a frequent topic of discussion in the United Nations and other international organizations, including the academic community, for more than three decades. The definition of this term has changed and today the most commonly used definition comes from the U.N. Brundtland Commission of the mid-1980s that defines sustainable development as meeting the needs of the present without compromising the ability of future generations to meet their needs.[21] Although this book purposefully tells the story of sustainable business from a developed nation (where the economy is dominated by industry) perspective, many innovative and powerful movement initiatives are currently underway inside developing nations. A discussion of the rich history and wide variety of approaches to sustainable business is worthy of a separate volume, and a number of literary works that have attempted to chronicle this phenomenon have been published.

The intention of the remainder of this section is to proffer some basic parameters for the continued evolution of sustainable business in developing nations by identifying common characteristics of previous positive efforts. In general, effective developing-world sustainable business initiatives have been organized and controlled by the local people themselves, have been compatible with local cultural traditions, and often have not been managed by outside interests. Developed-nation technology and process have been successfully imported into a region when the host community supports the arrangement and care is taken to respect the prevailing way of life.

The expression "Politics is always local"[22] parallels another statement in the context of developing nations, "Sustainable business is always local." Indeed, rather than seeing developing nations as simply market opportunities for our sustainable development ventures, a more effective and appropriately humble strategy would be to allow the citizens of these nations the dignity to choose and administer their own initiatives within the framework of their prevailing cultural components and natural-world setting. It is appropriate for each culture to independently define their concept of progress and to self-determine their manner of engagement of the sustainable business movement. Most folk cultures have a distinct and useful set of

---

[21] See Bruntland Commission (1987) for more about the United Nation's work with sustainable development.
[22] O'Neill and Hymel (1995).

traditions, which are demonstrated in many ways, including their architecture and communal functionality, around which intelligent adaptations and improvements can consolidate.

Citizens of developing nations have the opportunity to foster a fitting richness and diversity within their local adaptations of sustainable business principles. Africa, the least technologically advanced continent, is endowed with an abounding patchwork of mountains, jungles, plains, savannahs, coastlines, and deserts, along with hundreds of cultures and thousands of diverse communities. Quite possibly, the sustainable lifestyles and support structures that evolve across this landscape will be just as fitting for each locality as the indigenous natural communities that have occupied the land for many millennia. We can aspire for our movement leaders and organizations to avoid self-serving international promotion programs and to play a supporting role, however requested by the host community, in providing an appropriate contribution to their quest for durable opportunity and dignity. Just as movement participants slowly relinquish their illusion of dominion over the natural world, we have the opportunity to abandon the centuries-old presumption that technologically advanced nations have a duty to condescendingly subjugate the ideology of more primitive countries. Imported boiler-plate sustainable-development ventures that would benefit the developed world organization are rarely in the best interests of developing world society.

8.9 Back to the Front

From the opening paragraph in the introduction chapter, we have been on an intellectual and emotional rollercoaster ride. You have been asked to set aside foundational beliefs concerning business, the natural world, history, philosophy, education, and community and to read these pages with an open and contemplative mind. Beyond any particular principles of the movement, you were hopefully often inspired to think and reconsider, for this experience itself is intrinsically valuable. In a world that emphasizes self-gratification and compartmentalized knowledge, we are rarely prompted to examine our core beliefs and practices. If our foundational presumptions are shaky, then all that stands upon those beliefs are unsupported as well. Metaphorically, we may also find ourselves unaware of the forest, while extensively examining a single characteristic of a small tree.

In the beginning of our literary journey, you were promised a number of outcomes: a clear, thorough, and intriguing overview of the sustainable business movement; a unified and congruent body of thought; and solution-oriented systemic innovations. You were told that the movement would have direct applications to business reform and that numerous real-life examples of sustainable business practices would be discussed. You may have expected that both inspiration and practical steps for application would be part of the reading experience. I truly hope you were not disappointed.

The effectiveness of the numerous messages in this book is ultimately determined by you, the reader, both now and in the future. How well this work delivers on its promises is a question that only you can answer. My intention was to provide a useful guide that captures the full measure of potency for the steady progress of intelligent business and fecund communities in a variety of locations and situations. I hope this read was worth your time and effort and that you enjoyed the process. The road ahead is indeed daunting, but with each of us contributing our time, talents, and passion, the continuing journey is gloriously hopeful. As I often comment to my students and my audiences, if you find a better way to spend your professional time, please let me know and I will join you. So far, no appealing offer has emerged.

Guide Point 8: Although many obstacles lie ahead of the progression and coalescence of sustainable business, we have the ability to overcome each impediment and to bring this movement to complete fruition.

Bibliography

Benyus, J.M. (1997). *Biomimicry: Innovation Inspired by Nature*. New York: William Morrow and Company, Inc.

Braungart, M. and Engelfried, J. (1992). An "Intelligent Product System" to replace "Waste Management". *Fresenius Envir Bulletin*, 1, pp. 613–619.

Bruntland Commission (1987). *Our common Future*. United Nations World Commission on Environment and Development.

Costanza, R., d'Arge, R., de Goot, R., Farber, S., Grasso, M., Hannon, B., Limburg, K., Naeem, S., O'Neill, R.V. and Paruelo, J. (1997). The Value of the World's Ecosystem Services and Natural Capital. *Nature*, 387, pp. 253–260.

Cunningham, M., Houston, D. and Shepard, E. (2004). *The Andersonville Study of Retail Economics*. Civic Economics. Retrieved from http://www.andersonvillestudy.com/html/study.html.

Elkington, J. (1994). Towards the sustainable corporation: Win-win-win business strategies for sustainable development. *California Management Review*, 36(2), pp. 90–100.

Flader, S. and Callicott, J.B. (eds.). (1991). *The River of the Mother of God and Other Essays by Aldo Leopold*. Madison: University of Wisconsin Press.

Foskett, N. (1997). Teaching and learning through fieldwork. In Tilbury, D. and Wiliams M. (eds.), *Teaching and Learning Geography* (pp. 289–201). New York: Routledge.

Fuller, R.B. (1969). *Utopia or Oblivion: The Prospects for Humanity*. New York: Bantam Books.

Gershuny, J. (2003). Changing Times: Work and Leisure in Postindustrial Society. New York: Oxford University Press.

Hardin, G. (1968). Tragedy of the Commons. *Science*, 162, pp. 1243–1248.

Hawken, P. (1993). A Declaration of Sustainability. *Utne Reader*, pp. 54–61.

Hawken, P. (1993). *The Ecology of Commerce*. New York: Harper Collins.

Hawken, P., Lovins, A. and Lovins, L.H. (1999). *Natural Capitalism*. Boston: Little, Brown and Company.

Jacobs, A. and Gerson, K. (2001). Overworked individuals or overworked families? Explaining trends in work, leisure, and family time. *Work and Occupations*, 28, pp. 40–63.

King, D.A. (2004). The scientific impact of nations: What different countries get for their research spending. *Nature*, 430, pp. 311–316.

Leopold, A. (1949). *A Sand County Almanac and Sketches Here and There*. New York: Oxford University Press.

Leopold, A. (1938). Engineering and conservation. In Flader, S. and Callicott, J.B. (eds.) (1991), *The River of the Mother of God and Other Essays by Aldo Leopold*. Madison: University of Wisconsin Press.

Lisowski, M. and Disinger, J. (1991). The effects of field-based instruction on student understanding of ecological concepts. *Journal of Environmental Education*, 23, pp. 19–23.

McDonough, W. and Braungart M. (2002). *Cradle to Cradle: Remaking the Way We Make Things*. New York: North Point Press.

New Belgium Brewing Company (2008). *2007 Sustainability Report. 11.* Retrieved from http://www.newbelgium.com/files/shared/07SustainabilityReportlow.pdf.

O'Neill, T. and Hymel, G. (1995). *All Politics is Local: And Other Rules of the Game*. Cincinnati: Adams Media Corp.

Orion, M.R. and Hofstein, A. (1991). The measurement of students' attitudes towards scientific field trips. *Science Education*, 75, pp. 209–216.

Rebellato, L., Woods, W.I. and Na Neves, E.G. (2008). Pre-Columbian Dynamics in the Central Amazon. In *Amazonian Dark Earths: Wim Sombroek's Vision*. New York: Springer-Verlag.

Reguly, E. (2008, March 22). Lessons from Germany's energy renaissance. *The Globe and Mail*, B4.

Roberts, E.B. (2001). Benchmarking global strategic management of technology. *Research-Technology Management*, 44(2), pp. 25–36.

Schor, J. (1993). *The Overworked American: The Unexpected Decline of Leisure*. New York: Basic Books.

Teece, D.J. (2003). *Essays in Technology Management and Policy: Selected Papers of David J. Teece*. Singapore: World Scientific.

U.S. Environmental Protection Agency. (2008). *Atmosphere Changes*. Retrieved from http://www.epa.gov/climatechange/science/recentac.html.

Walker, C.H., Hopkin, S.P., Sibly, R.M. and Peakall, D.B. (2006). *Principles of Ecotoxicology*. London: Taylor & Francis, Inc.

Wilson, E.O. (1999). *Consilience — The Unity of Knowledge*. New York: Vintage.

Index

CPSIA information can be obtained at www.ICGtesting.com
Printed in the USA
BVOW06*0243240815

414726BV00005B/27/P